The College Admissions Process

Marcia Amidon Lusted, *Book Editor*

GREENHAVEN PUBLISHING

Published in 2018 by Greenhaven Publishing, LLC
353 3rd Avenue, Suite 255, New York, NY 10010

Articles in Greenhaven Publishing anthologies are often edited for length to meet page requirements. In addition, original titles of these works are changed to clearly present the main thesis and to explicitly indicate the author's opinion. Every effort is made to ensure that Greenhaven Publishing accurately reflects the original intent of the authors. Every effort has been made to trace the owners of the copyrighted material.

Library of Congress Cataloging-in-Publication Data

Names: Lusted, Marcia Amidon, editor.
Title: The college admissions process / Marcia Amidon Lusted, book editor.
Description: First edition. I New York : Greenhaven Publishing, 2018. I Series: Issues that concern you I Includes bibliographical references and index. I Audience: Grade 9–12.
Identifiers: LCCN 2017034174 I ISBN 9781534502239 (library bound) I ISBN 9781534502819 (paperback)
Subjects: LCSH: Universities and colleges—United States—Admission—Juvenile literature.
Classification: LCC LB2351.2 .C635 2018 I DDC 378.1/61—dc23
LC record available at https://lccn.loc.gov/2017034174

Manufactured in the United States of America

Website: http://greenhavenpublishing.com

CONTENTS

One of the biggest tasks that many American high school students go through in their junior and senior years is the process of applying to colleges. In the 1960s and 1970s, the requirements for students who wanted to get into a good college were fairly simple: 1) high school graduation; 2) a minimum number of classes in certain subjects; 3) student rank in graduating class; 4) recommendation of the principal; 5) a personal interview; and 6) aptitude and achievement test scores. Most students applied to three or four colleges because applications required paper forms and handwritten essays and took time and effort.

In the last forty or fifty years, however, the scenario for students applying and being accepted at colleges has changed drastically. In 1960, 45 percent of high school graduates applied to and were accepted in colleges. By 1998, that number had grown to 65 percent and was also based on a larger population of high school students. There are simply more students applying to colleges, which makes the admission process more competitive. Students are being asked to identify potential careers in middle school and take aptitude tests to help them identify their strongest possible fields of study. Students are also taught early on that an education from a top, very selective school will help them achieve excellent careers and high paychecks, so the push is there to try for these extremely selective schools.

Many students now apply to colleges that they don't even have much of a chance of getting in to, based on their academic records, but they still try. This clogs the application process and skews the acceptance rate for prestigious schools. And with more and more competition for the few slots at especially selective schools, like Harvard, Yale, Dartmouth, Vassar, and other Ivy League schools, an entire industry developed around helping students get into colleges and universities. Today students enroll in prep classes for the Scholastic Aptitude Test (SAT), go to private tutors to help them write their college admissions essays, and sometimes even have private coaches who help them through the entire process.

In addition, students have many more recommendations for what they should do to make themselves appeal to college admissions committees. They participate in extracurricular activities and community service, they take Advanced Placement (AP) courses during high school, and they participate in enrichment activities in the arts or sciences or other areas that make them stand out from other applicants.

On top of this, students are applying to more colleges than they used to: today many students apply to ten or fifteen schools. It has become easier to apply to multiple colleges because all applications are done online, and many use the Common Application, a universal application that can be filled out once by the student and then submitted to many different schools.

The combination of these factors, and the competition for schools with good reputations, creates huge amounts of stress for high school students. They must spend long hours studying, especially if they are taking Advanced Placement courses or honors-level classes, but also participate in extracurricular and community activities. These workloads are in addition to whatever other normal activities students have to juggle, such as working part-time jobs, helping with family responsibilities such as babysitting or caring for a sick family member, helping with a family-owned business, or participating in church or club activities. This not only puts pressure on students, but it makes the stakes much higher. A student who has been doing everything possible to appear to be a good candidate for schools to accept into their freshman classes can be devastated and depressed if they don't get into their first choice—or even top choices—of schools.

In addition, high school guidance counselors, who should be available to help students make some of the biggest decisions of their lives, are often faced with the burden of too many students to help and not enough time or resources to do so. According to an article in the *Atlantic*:

> [College admissions is] a mania to which more and more teens are subjecting themselves, pressuring applicants to pad their resumés and tout superficial experiences and hobbies,

convincing them that attending a prestigious school is paramount. And critics say that mania has even spread into and shaped American culture, often distorting kids' (and parents') values, perpetuating economic inequality, and perverting the role of higher education in society as a whole.[1]

All this might make it seem that getting into a good college is becoming more and more difficult, if not impossible. But things are improving, according to many education experts. Demographics are changing in favor of high school seniors. There just aren't as many graduating seniors each year as there were between 1990 and 2011. In 2011, the number of high school seniors peaked at about 3.4 million graduates, and since then it has continued to fall slightly to 3.3 million graduates a year in 2014. It is expected to begin to climb again starting around the year 2020. This means, simply, that fewer students are applying for college slots. Some colleges are even increasing the sizes of their freshman classes, so there are more slots open to applicants. Colleges are also making changes to their admissions processes and criteria. They are trying to accommodate students who are smart but not good at taking standardized tests like the SAT or ACT. They are also trying to make applications fair for students who can't afford to pay the application fees or who come from disadvantaged backgrounds.

A college education is a benefit that students will use throughout their lives. It is one of the best ways to achieve upward mobility for underprivileged students. It is the pathway to a good job. The college application process may be stressful and complicated for many schools, but for other options such as community colleges or smaller, less prestigious colleges and universities, the process can be easier and much less stressful. When students finally receive their college diploma, what matters isn't so much which school they receive it from, but how much they invested emotionally and intellectually in achieving their own education.

Notes

1. "The Absurdity of College Admissions," by Alia Wong, *Atlantic*, March 28, 2016. https://www.theatlantic.com/education/archive/2016/03/where-admissions-went-wrong/475575

ONE

The College Admissions Process Is Too Stressful for Teens

Michelle Trudeau

In the following viewpoint, Michelle Trudeau argues that the pressures and workloads that teens take on in order to get into good colleges are taking a toll on their health. Many are suffering from stress, anxiety, and depression. Trudeau uses quotes from parents and students who are in the middle of the college admissions process. She also quotes experts from the health profession, as well as college admissions professionals. Trudeau is a science reporter and producer for NPR's Science Desk. Her news reports and feature stories, which cover the areas of human behavior, child development, the brain sciences, and mental health, air on NPR's *Morning Edition* and *All Things Considered* programs.

This is the season of college applications and high-stakes entrance exams. Tens of thousands of teenagers are pushing hard to do well. Many, though, are overworked, overscheduled and overstressed—and it's taking a toll on the mental health and development of a number of teens.

The American Academy of Pediatrics is sounding the alarm in a new report. The report emphasizes that the majority of teens are doing just fine, despite the intense pressure and fully booked schedules. But adolescent-medicine specialist Kenneth Ginsburg,

Many teens find themselves overwhelmed by the stress of maintaining good grades and participating in extracurricular activities, never mind the college application process itself.

who authored the report, says more and more teens are being sidelined by anxiety and depression.

The Race to Prepare

Marilee Jones is the mother of a teenager and the dean of admissions at MIT. Personally and professionally, she understands exactly what Ginsburg is talking about.

Jones vividly recalls a moment when her daughter, now a college freshman, was in 7th grade.

"I remember [telling] her she has to get ready for high school, she needs to develop activities, she needs to have interests, she needs to develop passions," Jones says. "And I remember that she looked at me like she had no idea what I was talking about. And really, within a few months, she started having stomach pain."

The doctor told Jones that stress might be the culprit. "And that there was nothing wrong with her," Jones says. "It was all coming from me."

From her own parenting experience as well as from interviewing thousands of teens for college admission, Jones has come to the conclusion that our children are under way too much pressure. They're far too busy—and highly stressed—all in the service of getting into college.

"I've been in school for three weeks and already it's really hectic, because you get thrown into all this college stuff," says Tom Poulis, a senior at University High School in Southern California. "And people are always telling you, 'Apply here.' And when are you going to take your SATs? And on top of that I'm taking four AP classes. So already, the stress level is very high."

Then there are his extracurricular activities. Poulis is president of the debate club, an officer with Amnesty International, and a student representative on the Associated Student Body Cabinet, to name a few.

Poulis is certain that colleges are looking for hard-working, fully committed students. But he's not just trying to rev up his resume. He says he enjoys all his activities and courses. And he gets no pressure from his parents to carry such a large load.

Like Tom, Rachel Ferrell is in 12th grade. She loves high school so much that when she wakes up in the morning, she actually wants to go to school.

Nevertheless, the race has begun.

Stress Reduction

"We have to start looking at scholarships and we have to start narrowing down our schools that we want to go to and looking at deadlines," Ferrell says. "Because there's a lot of deadlines, like in

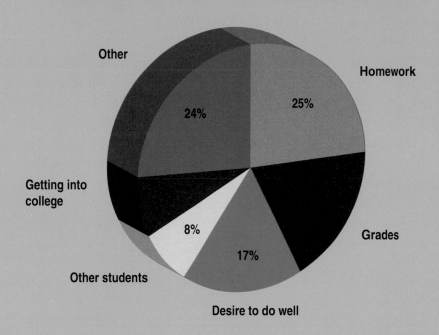

Primary causes of stress among high school students

Other
24%

Homework
25%

Getting into college

Grades

8%

17%

Other students

Desire to do well

Source: The Princeton Review

November, if you want to do early decision or early action, or get financial aid, or whatever."

Ferrell thinks she wants to go into the arts but hasn't yet decided where she'll apply.

"And I'm freaking out because of the money," she says. "It's just so expensive to go to school. I mean, $40,000! It's just so ridiculously overpriced."

Chelsea Halprin, a junior, hopes to apply to Columbia or Harvard. She has a nonstop schedule: homework, class president, team sports, mentoring younger students, helping at her synagogue. But she worries that in spite of all she does, it might not be enough.

And she has a point.

"This is sort of the peak of the demographics," says Marilee Jones, the MIT dean of admissions. "So when people feel anxious about the competition and worry that, 'Oh no, there are just so many people applying to college,' they're right. That's a true anxiety they feel."

That anxiety can take a toll on health, says adolescent medicine specialist Ginsburg. He sees many teenagers whose bodies show the signs of stress, whether it's headaches or chest pain or belly pain.

"At the extreme—and I want to emphasize that this is the extreme—we're seeing more kids who are engaging in self-mutilation," Ginsburg says. "[It's] a way of taking control over their life when they feel their life is out of control. And I see quite a few kids with eating disorders. It's kids who just feel like they can't handle everything they're doing."

There are other, less obvious concerns. Jones believes that creativity and innovative thinking are taking a hit.

"Because students are so busy all the time, because parents think that's what they need to get into college, and we in college admissions officers reinforce that, they don't get into their imagination enough," Jones says.

Her remedy: "Let's free up a lot of kids to be able to do that and not force everybody to have all of those AP classes and all of those activities."

Meanwhile, the stress just keeps on mounting. "One of my friends," says Poulis, "She just one day was like, 'I'm tired of school. I'm tired of feeling bad about having, like, a 3.6 GPA. Tired of being in an environment that demands so much of you. And tired of an environment where the level of your character is determined by your SAT score.'"

To help teenagers cope, the American Academy of Pediatrics is launching a new Web site where teens can go and design their own stress-reduction plans, described by the doctors as a "prescription for balance."

TWO

There Isn't Room
for Everyone

Ben Jones

In the following viewpoint, Ben Jones offers a perspective from the admissions side of the college application process. He discusses from his own personal experience the detailed and painstaking process of what happens when applications are received by admissions officers. He also emphasizes how many qualified student applicants he sees every day and how few the college can actually accept. While this can be perceived as cold by applicants, who have worked hard to do everything right, the truth is that admissions committees invest a tremendous amount of effort and emotion in selecting their classes. From 2004–2008 Jones was director of communications for the MIT office of admissions. His job included reading applications and selecting students for admission to MIT. He is now vice president for communications at Oberlin College.

In response to an earlier entry of mine, this post appeared on College Confidential:

> You know, I get sick of college admissions officers saying how they couldn't accept so many wonderful people. While it's supposed to be comforting, obviously, I just find it really insincere. I mean, either you're accepted or you're not. There is no grey area...so they shouldn't try to sugarcoat the harsh reality.

"It's More Than A Job," by Ben Jones, Massachusetts Institute of Technology, March 17, 2006. Reprinted by permission.

Colleges and universities invest a great deal of time and effort into deciding whom they will accept.

I'm thankful to whomever posted this, because it really made me think. It's certainly a fair post, and I imagine a lot of our applicants share these sentiments. A million years ago when I was applying to college, perhaps I would have felt the same way.

I've written before about how the class is selected, but I'm too tired to dig up the post so I'll give a quick recap. First you apply. Your application is read by a senior staff member who will look for deal-breakers (like a bunch of D's, for example). Assuming you're competitive, your application is then read by a primary reader who will summarize it at length for the committee. Then a second reader (and sometimes a third) will read and write their own summaries. Then it will go to selection committee, where multiple groups of different admissions staff and faculty members will weigh in on it. Assuming you've made it that far, the senior staff will then review it *again*. Approximately 12 people (give or take) will significantly discuss and debate your application before you're admitted. This is all very intentional; committee decisions ensure that every decision is correct in the context of the overall applicant pool, and that no one individual's bias or preferences or familiarity with a given case has any chance of swaying a decision unfairly.

With that in mind, let me tell you a little bit about what my job is like from November through March. Three days a week, I take a random bunch of applications to the public library, find a quiet corner, and immerse myself in your lives.

I read about your triumphs, I read about your dreams, I read about the tragedies that define you. I read about your passions, your inventions, your obsession with video games, dance, Mozart, Monet. I read about the person close to you who died. I read about your small towns, your big cities, the week you spent abroad that changed your life. I read about your parents getting divorced, your house burning down, your girlfriend cheating on you. I read about the car you rebuilt with your dad, the championship debate you lost, the team you led to failure, the performance you aced. I read about the people you've helped and the people you've hurt. I read about how you've stood tall in the face of racism, homophobia, poverty, injustice.

Then I read about the lives you've changed—a math or science teacher, a humanities teacher, a counselor. I read the things that they probably don't say to your face for fear of inflating your ego: that you're the best in their careers, that kids like you are the reason they chose to be a teacher in the first place, that they're better people for having known you.

If you've had an interview, I get to read about how you come across in person to someone you've just met—how your face lights

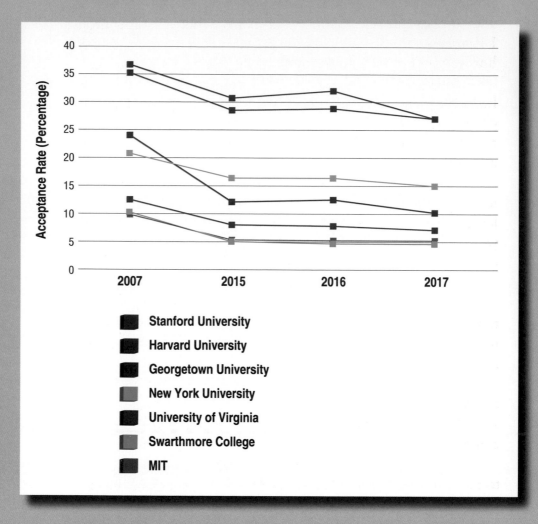

Acceptance rates among select top US colleges and universities, 2007–2017

Acceptance Rate (Percentage)

40
35
30
25
20
15
10
5
0

2007   2015   2016   2017

■ Stanford University
■ Harvard University
■ Georgetown University
■ New York University
■ University of Virginia
■ Swarthmore College
■ MIT

Source: IvyWise

up at the mention of cell biology, how you were five minutes late because you had an audition, how your smile can fill a room, how you simply *shine*.

(Your grades and scores are clearly competitive or your application wouldn't be on my pile in the first place.)

By now I'm fully invested in you so I write a gazillion nice things about you in your summary and I'm smiling the whole time. I talk about your depth, all the ways you're a great match to MIT, all the things I know you'll contribute to campus. I conclude with phrases like "clear admit" and "perfect choice." In my head I imagine bumping into you on the Infinite Corridor, asking you how your UROP is going, seeing your a cappella group perform.

I come home each night and tell my wife over dinner how lucky I am, because I never seem to pick boring applications out of the pile. In fact, I tell her, I'm inspired enough by the stories I read to think that the world might actually turn out to be okay after all.

In March I go into committee with my colleagues, having narrowed down my top picks to a few hundred people. My colleagues have all done the same. Then the numbers come in: *this year's admit rate will be 13%. For every student you admit, you need to let go of seven others.*

What? But I have so many who...*But*...

And then the committee does its work, however brutal. It's not pretty, but at least it's fair. (And by fair I mean fair in the context of the applicant pool; of course it's not fair that there are so few spots for so many qualified applicants.)

When it's all over, about 13% of my top picks are offered admission. I beg, I plead, I make ridiculous promises (just ask the senior staff) but at the end of the day, a committee decision is a committee decision.

Of my many favorites this year, there were a few who really got to me, and when they didn't get in, the tears came. Some would call me foolish for getting this wrapped up in the job, but honestly, I couldn't do this job if I disconnected myself from the human component of it. It's my job to present you to the committee; if your dream of being at MIT didn't become *my* dream on some small level, then really, why am I doing this at all? Others would disagree, but then, others aren't me.

To the 87% of you who have shared your lives with us and trusted us with your stories over the last four months, please know that they meant something to me, and I won't forget you. When I say that I share the pain of these decisions with you, I'm not lying. I'm really not lying.

To the person up there who said "while it's supposed to be comforting, obviously, I just find it really insincere"—you have it backwards. I don't expect it (or anything else) to be comforting at this moment. But insincere? No. Not that.

Just got confirmation that the USPS picked up the mail (for real), so it's on the way. I'll be thinking about all of you.

THREE

Colleges Should Be Able to Practice Race-Conscious Admissions

Liliana M. Garces

> In the following viewpoint, Liliana M. Garces argues that colleges must work hard to commit to admitting a racially and ethnically diverse body of students. Even though race-conscious admissions are protected by law, colleges are under constant threat of facing race-related legal challenges. Some schools are more financially protected than others in dealing with such challenges, and a college's endowment has been proved to directly factor into the diversity of its student body. The author emphasizes the importance of creating an environment of diversity, which benefits all students. Garces is an associate professor at the University of Texas at Austin and an affiliate faculty member at the University of Texas School of Law. Her research focuses on inequities in education.

L ast summer, the Supreme Court ruled that colleges and universities can use race as one factor among many in making admissions decisions. The court determined that such policies helped further an institution's mission to attain the educational benefits of diversity.

A recent report by the *New York Times*, however, has brought affirmative action back to the forefront. According to the *New York Times*, the Trump administration may be considering a

Supporters of affirmative action believe that it's still the best way to ensure a diverse student body, something that benefits all students.

"project" to direct Department of Justice resources to investigate race-conscious admissions. While Department of Justice officials responded that the internal memo did not reflect new department policy, the story has placed colleges and universities "on notice" that their efforts may face renewed scrutiny.

As an education and legal scholar of equity in higher education, I've represented hundreds of social scientists before the Supreme Court to support colleges' use of race-conscious admissions. My belief—and that of many educators and civil rights advocates— is that the alleged investigation by the Department of Justice is meant to intimidate institutions and, perhaps, sway admissions officers from considering race in their admissions policies.

Unintentional or not, the potential threat of legal action could have a dramatic impact on the diversity of college campuses across the country.

Legal Intimidation

Despite the Supreme Court's ruling last year, conservative groups like Students for Fair Admissions continue to press lawsuits against universities that employ race-conscious admissions. Cases against Harvard University and UNC Chapel Hill are making their way through the courts and could potentially bring affirmative action to the Supreme Court again.

However, Harvard and Chapel Hill have some of the largest endowments in the country, with US$34 billion and $2 billion, respectively. Might institutions that lack the financial resources to defend against lawsuits begin changing admissions policies and practices in order to avoid potential legal threats?

A recent study found that over the last 20 years, a public commitment to race-conscious admissions has become far less common, particularly among institutions that are relatively lower in the status hierarchy. In 1994, 82 percent of "very competitive" public universities openly considered race as one of many factors in admissions decisions. By 2014, that number declined to just 32 percent. The "most competitive" universities, however, have continued their public commitment to race-conscious admissions practices unabated.

While the reasons for this trend haven't been studied directly, it's worth noting that the "most competitive" institutions are also the institutions that have more financial resources to defend against potential legal action.

Why Opposition Exists

In many ways, higher education provides a pathway to positions of power and influence in the United States.

Attending an elite institution remains an important part of the trajectory for those in the ruling class. Harvard, Stanford and

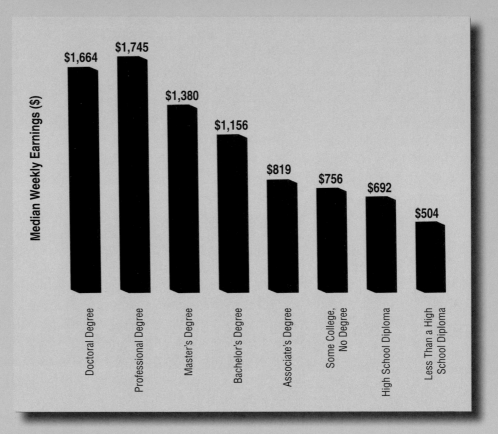

Earnings by educational attainment, 2016

Median Weekly Earnings ($)

- Doctoral Degree — $1,664
- Professional Degree — $1,745
- Master's Degree — $1,380
- Bachelor's Degree — $1,156
- Associate's Degree — $819
- Some College, No Degree — $756
- High School Diploma — $692
- Less Than a High School Diploma — $504

Source: Bureau of Labor

Yale, for example, have graduated considerably more recent members of Congress than other less prestigious schools.

Elite institutions also provide particularly high labor market returns for students of color. Economists have shown, for example, that attending the most selective institutions made an especially big difference in the life earnings for black, Latino and first-generation students.

Keeping the path to high-status positions open for people of color was one of the reasons the Supreme Court found race-conscious admissions to be constitutional. In the words of the court, to cultivate a set of leaders with legitimacy in the eyes of the citizenry, "the path to leadership must be visibly open to talented and qualified individuals of every race and ethnicity."

A recent opinion piece by Emory professor Carol Anderson made the compelling case for why opposition to affirmative action is grounded on the politics of white resentment—that is, a false view that opening the path to the ruling class for black and Latino students represents a "theft" of those resources from white students.

A World Without Affirmative Action

What happens when colleges and universities cannot consider race as a factor in admissions?

Research shows that, without race-conscious admissions, the racial diversity of student bodies drops substantially. For example, African-American and Latino enrollment declined at the most selective undergraduate institutions in states with bans on affirmative action. Similar findings were reported in enrollment at law schools and business schools after these bans were instituted.

My own research documents declines due to affirmative action bans across a number of graduate fields of study, including engineering and natural and social sciences as well as medical schools.

The decline in racial diversity across these educational sectors exacerbates the already disproportionately low number of students of color in these programs and reduces the variety of perspectives that are needed to foster innovation and advance scientific inquiry.

In short, race-conscious admissions do make a difference in campus diversity, allowing universities to address, rather than exacerbate, existing racial inequities.

Next Steps for Universities

Though the Fisher case cleared a path for race-conscious admissions, universities must still do their part. The court ruled that institutions must be able to connect racial and ethnic diversity to their mission and demonstrate why so-called "race-neutral" efforts are not as effective as race-conscious ones.

However, these steps alone are not enough for preserving true diversity in the face of ongoing attacks.

One of the very important aspects of the Fisher decision is that the Court's rationale reflects a robust understanding of diversity: namely, that diversity is about more than the number of students of color; it's also about fostering an environment in which students can benefit from diversity.

Research suggests that this means ensuring that students are engaging across racial and ethnic lines. In an analysis of decades of social science research, my co-author and I learned that realizing the benefits of diversity requires healthy, even if uncomfortable, cross-racial interactions.

Doing so requires attending to the ways that race, in explicit and subconscious ways, influences our interactions and shapes educational opportunity. It's hard to see how institutions can do so without considering race in their educational policies and practices—including college admissions.

FOUR

Race-Based Decisions Don't Help Anyone in the Long Run

Jennifer Gratz

> Affirmative action is a policy that favors or provides opportunities to members of groups who have been historically discriminated against. In the following excerpted viewpoint, Jennifer Gratz argues that college admissions candidates are often judged on their eligibility for acceptance based on skin color, rather than on their accomplishments and potential. At some schools, students who fall into certain racial categories are evaluated on a different system than those who do not meet those categories. Gratz uses examples from students on both sides of the racial discrimination issue. Gratz was part of two Supreme Court cases that ultimately banned preferential treatment based on race, gender, ethnicity, or national origin. Currently, she works for the American Civil Rights Institute.

When it comes to typical "reverse discrimination" cases, many people know high-profile stories like mine and that of Frank Ricci. For instance, my story made national headlines when I challenged the University of Michigan's decision to use skin color as the primary basis for rejecting my application for admission.

At the time of my application, the university reviewed applications submitted by black, Native American, and Hispanic applicants under one standard and those submitted by everyone else

"Discriminating Toward Equality: Affirmative Action and the Diversity Charade," by Jennifer Gratz, The Heritage Foundation, February 27, 2014. Reprinted by permission.

under a much higher standard.[1] The school later claimed to simplify the admissions process by using a point system and automatically awarding an extra 20 points (out of 100) to select minorities. By comparison, a perfect SAT score earned an applicant only 12 points. Thus, even though I had good grades and a host of extracurricular activities, the university rejected my application because I had the wrong skin color. My case, *Gratz v. Bollinger*,[2] ultimately went before the Supreme Court, and in 2003, the Court ruled that racial discrimination had indeed taken place.

Proponents of reverse discrimination often argue that only privileged white individuals have any reason to oppose the use of racial preferences. These diversity engineers believe the benefits of expanding opportunities to certain minorities far outweigh the costs of using race to treat people differently. However, the personal stories of those who have been adversely affected by these policies—both the traditional victims and even the supposed beneficiaries—paint a very different picture. The following are just a few of them.[3]

The Stigma of Affirmative Action

Ashley graduated from high school at 16 years of age with a 4.3 GPA and scored a 32 on the ACT.[4] She was active in numerous extracurricular activities and, not surprisingly, was accepted into every college to which she applied. Ashley did not want racial admissions boosts, and she did not need them. She knew, however, that she would get them anyway because she happened to be black. Despite her hard work and impressive accomplishments, she feared ever having a bad day or getting an answer wrong in class lest her peers think she got accepted only because of her skin color.

The use of race-conscious admissions policies at her university saddled Ashley with an unwanted stigma based on her skin color. It reinforced stereotypes of inequality and special treatment, forcing her constantly to feel the need to prove that she deserved to be in the classroom. Rather than helping Ashley, racial preferences obscured the legitimacy of her achievements. She wanted

Are race-conscious admissions policies actually detrimental to students—even to those they are intended to help?

to be judged as an individual; instead, she worked twice as hard to overcome being judged for her skin color. Recently, the University of Michigan's Black Student Union received national attention when its "Being Black at the University of Michigan" hashtag went viral on Twitter. Hundreds of students joined in to share the "unique experiences of being black at Michigan."[5] The vast majority of the comments were negative, and almost every single one of the students who commented expressed frustration with being treated differently because of his or her skin color. The students' demand that they be treated as unique individuals—instead of as token members of racial or ethnic groups—was striking, and it highlighted the fact that putting people in boxes and discriminating based on appearance is demeaning, harmful, and wrong. Is it any less so when it is done by public officials and administrators?

The "Wrong" Kind of Minority

David, a student living in Los Angeles, wanted to attend the University of California, Los Angeles, but was rejected despite excellent grades and test scores.[6] David happened to be Vietnamese and was held to a much higher admission standard because of his ethnicity. Even being a minority applicant won him no favor in the system of discrimination for the sake of diversity. In the interest of maintaining a diverse campus, the university chose to limit the number of high-performing Asian enrollees. He was told he should accept discrimination for the "common good" and that he could always attend another elite school. For David, however, racial discrimination forced him to choose between taking care of his immobile grandmother and moving out-of-state to further his education.

Barbara Grutter, the mother of two sons, applied to the University of Michigan Law School in 1996.[7] Before applying, she had started a successful business, had graduated from Michigan State with a 3.8 GPA and high honors, and had scored 161 on the LSAT. She also happened to be white. The law school initially placed Barbara on their waiting list but later rejected her. Only 20 percent of white and Asian students with similar marks got into the school; however, "underrepresented" minorities with the same grades had a 100 percent acceptance rate.

Why the disparity? The law school gave preferences to certain applicants based on skin color. Grutter decided to sue, and in the course of the court hearings and testimony, it became clear that race accounted for well over a quarter of applicants' admission scores. Unfortunately, in 2003, the Supreme Court, in *Grutter v. Bollinger*, upheld the school's racially discriminatory policies as necessary for achieving the goals of a diverse campus.[8] The Court's holding was based on the flimsy rationale that because

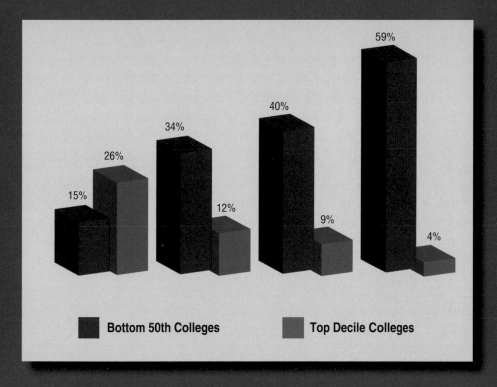

Percentage of students from four racial backgrounds enrolled at top decile and bottom fiftieth colleges, 2013

- 15%
- 26%
- 34%
- 12%
- 40%
- 9%
- 59%
- 4%

■ Bottom 50th Colleges   ■ Top Decile Colleges

Source: Department of Education

the preferences were not codified into a point system, they were permissible as part of a "holistic" admissions process.

Barbara entered the workforce in the 1970s along with many other women "empowered and emboldened by the belief that equal opportunity meant that it was illegal to judge anyone on the basis of race, gender, or anything else that has nothing to do with one's abilities."[9] She feared this newfound opportunity would prove illusory and that it could be "pulled back" at any moment, which is ultimately what happened—because of her race.

Experts insisted that racial preferences and the pursuit of diversity were good for Barbara and society as a whole. She could always attend another law school, they argued. Yet none of these experts discussed the fact that Barbara was only interested in attending a well-respected law school and, as a mother of two young children, was unable to move out-of-state to attend other schools. The University of Michigan was her only real option, but she was denied admission because of her race.

Katuria Smith grew up in poverty.[10] She was born when her mother was 17, had an alcoholic father and stepfather, dropped out of high school, and survived on any menial job she could find. By the time she turned 21 years old, Katuria was desperate to escape poverty, so she took night classes at a community college paralegal program while juggling jobs during the day. She graduated and enrolled in the University of Washington where she earned a degree.

With her 3.65 GPA and LSAT score of 165, Katuria applied to the University of Washington School of Law. Considering her background, she expected to be admitted. Instead, her application was rejected.

In order to bolster campus diversity, the university used race as a factor in determining whom to admit to its law school, maintaining separate admissions standards and procedures for minority applicants. The dean later admitted that with her story and qualifications, Katuria would have been accepted had she been a member of a "preferred" racial group.[11] The university claimed they employed a "holistic" approach in the admissions process, but even Katuria's incredible life story of overcoming remarkable hurdles was not enough to make up for the fact that she was not the right color. In the end, a "holistic" admission proved to be mostly about race.

The Double Standard

Lee Bollinger is a prominent supporter of racial preferences and a self-proclaimed champion of diversity and equal opportunity. He was president of the University of Michigan when Barbara and I filed our lawsuits, and he publicly supported the university's right to use race-based preferences throughout the legal proceedings. To him, a 20 percent boost for race meant "one of many factors," and selectively distributing special treatment based on race was consistent with equal protection under the law.

Now the president of Columbia University, Mr. Bollinger recently dealt with a new discrimination matter—a "whites only" scholarship fund established by a wealthy divorcée days before her death in 1920.[12] Bollinger is seeking a court order to lift the race restrictions because of the ugliness of discrimination, but he has remained silent on the long list of scholarships Columbia promotes only for "students of color." In the eyes of Bollinger and those who agree with his position, preferential treatment counts as discrimination only when the race in question is not currently favored by the government or those in academia's ivory towers.

President Obama on Affirmative Action

When the Michigan Civil Rights Initiative appeared on the ballot in 2006, then-Senator Barack Obama recorded a radio ad urging viewers to vote against it.[13] He insisted that by not allowing policies that grant special treatment based on skin color, Michigan would undermine equal opportunity and reverse racial progress.

Just a year later, ABC News' George Stephanopoulos asked Senator Obama whether his daughters should receive special treatment because of their race when applying to college.[14] Obama said his two daughters "should probably be treated by any admissions officer as folks who are pretty advantaged"—a subtle acknowledgment of the absurdity of using race to determine preferential treatment. While his daughters may share the same skin color as a child in inner-city Chicago, their backgrounds are worlds apart. In today's increasingly pluralistic society, race usually does not—and certainly should not—determine what obstacles individuals have had to overcome or advantages they have received.

A Legacy of Discrimination

There are four important lessons to draw from the stories recounted above.

Racial preferences are a form of discrimination. Any time an individual is granted preferential treatment based on race, opportunities are denied to others who may be just as qualified or needy but who simply have the "wrong" skin color or are the wrong gender. The government's preference for one race (or gender or ethnicity) over another is the very definition of discrimination. Regardless of intentions, such policies create new injustices with new victims. No one—white, black, Asian, Latino, Native American, or any other color or ethnicity—should be turned away from education, scholarships, jobs, contracts, or promotions because they have the "wrong" skin color. This kind of discrimination was wrong 50 years ago, and it is still wrong today.

Racial preferences rob recipients of the pride of ownership in their accomplishments. When individuals of a certain race are selected to receive special treatment, those individuals must struggle against the idea that their skin color rather than merit is behind their success. Indeed, the achievements of people like Ashley, who did not need or want preferences, will forever be judged through the lens of racial preferences.

The values of the diversity movement are only skin deep. Proponents of these reverse discrimination policies refuse to treat people as individuals. Instead, they rely on discriminatory stereotypes and gross generalizations to label, judge, and group people based on race, gender, and ethnicity. Individuals are reduced to a skin color or gender type because diversity's champions have little patience for the actual work needed to promote real diversity. Ask a university president how many black students are on campus, and he or she will be able to provide the number on the spot. But ask about the number of musicians, conservatives, liberals, libertarians, or students from single-parent homes, and he or she will be at a loss to provide any meaningful statistics. Real diversity is found in the wealth of experience, talents, perspectives, and interests of unique individuals. People of the same race do not all think alike.

Race-based policies force people to make decisions and judgments that do not reflect how people live their lives. The average person thinks very little about race on a daily basis, yet the diversity culture and racial preference policies insist that race is the centerpiece of almost every issue, work environment, and educational experience. People are constantly forced to describe themselves by checking a box or choosing a label from a list of predetermined and frequently artificial categories. From an early age, children are taught not to judge a person based on appearance, but when they grow older, they learn that this is exactly what is happening and being encouraged all around them.

America is ready to move beyond race. However, if the government and public institutions continue to divide the country by ethnicity and race, the goal of a color-blind society will remain beyond our reach. Policies that promote race-based discrimination continue to undermine the American Dream, and the only way to end the vicious cycle of discrimination is to ensure that fair and equal treatment for everyone is a reality, not just a talking point.

Notes

1. Center for Individual Rights, Charting Racial Discrimination, http://www .cir-usa.org/cases/michigan_lsa_charts.html (last visited Feb. 7, 2014) (the guidelines used by the University of Michigan's undergraduate admissions office).

2. 539 U.S. 244 (2003).

3. Some names have been changed to protect privacy.

4. Videotape: Adam Abraham, An Act of Courage (American Civil Rights Coalition 2004) (on file with author). Ashley is featured in this video.

5. Rhonesha Byng, *#BBUM Hashtag Sparks Dialogue About Diversity at the University of Michigan*, Huffington Post, Nov. 20, 2013, *available at* http:// www.huffingtonpost.com/2013/11/20/bbum-university-of-michigan-black -students_n_4310790.html?ncid=txtlnkushpmg00000038.

6. Interview with Jennifer Gratz.

7. News Conference, Center for Individual Rights, Supreme Court Affirmative Action Cases (Mar. 31, 2003), *available at* http://www.c-spanvideo.org/program /CourtAf.

8. 539 U.S. 306 (2003).

9. News Conference, *supra* note 11.

10. Center for Individual Rights, Smith v. University of Washington, http:// www.cir-usa.org/cases/smith.html (last visited Feb. 7, 2014) (a compilation of documents related to Katuria's lawsuit).

11. Nat Hentoff, *Katuria Smith Goes to Court*, Village Voice, July 8, 1998, *available at* http://www.cir-usa.org/articles/140.html. 12. Sharyn Jackson, *Whites-only Scholarship at Columbia Challenged*, USA Today, May 15, 2013, *available at* http://www.usatoday.com/story/news/nation/2013/05/15/whites-only-scholarship-challenged/2164815.

13. Stephen Hayes, *The Race Minefield*, Weekly Standard, Mar. 10, 2008, *available at* http://www.weeklystandard.com/Content/Public/Articles/000/000/014/823xthib.asp?pg=1#.

14. Eugene Robinson, *A Question of Race v. Class*, Wash. Post, May 15, 2007, *available at* http://www.washingtonpost.com/wp-dyn/content/article/2007/05/14/AR2007051401233.html.

FIVE

We Need to Be Careful About the Standardized Tests We Choose

Richard C. Atkinson

Standardized tests are still a substantial measure in the college admissions process, but their merits are under debate. In the following excerpted viewpoint, Richard Atkinson argues that students should be selected on the basis of the success they have demonstrated in learning, rather than on their aptitude on standardized tests. The author touches on several different forms of standardized testing and makes a case for which ones are actually the best indicators of a student's ability to be successful in college. Atkinson is president emeritus of the University of California and professor emeritus of cognitive science and psychology at the University of California, San Diego. He is a former director of the National Science Foundation and was a long-term member of the faculty at Stanford University.

In a democratic society, I argued, admitting students to a college or university should be based on three principles. First, students should be judged on the basis of their actual achievements, not on ill-defined notions of aptitude. Second, standardized tests should have a demonstrable relationship to the specific subjects taught in high school, so that students can use the tests to assess their mastery of those subjects. Third, U.S. universities should employ

"Achievement Versus Aptitude in College Admissions," by Richard C. Atkinson, University of Texas at Dallas, 2002. Reprinted by permission.

Grades and test scores are not the only factors in college admissions. It is important to participate in community outreach programs.

admissions processes that look at individual applicants in their full complexity and take special pains to ensure that standardized tests are used properly in admissions decisions. I'd like to discuss each in turn.

Aptitude versus Achievement

Aptitude tests such as the SAT I have a historical tie to the concept of innate mental abilities and the belief that such abilities can be defined and meaningfully measured. Neither notion has been supported by modern research. Few scientists who have considered these matters seriously would argue that aptitude tests such as the SAT I provide a true measure of intellectual abilities.

Nonetheless, the SAT I is widely regarded as a test of basic mental ability that can give us a picture of students' academic promise. Those who support it do so in the belief that it helps guarantee that the students admitted to college will be highly qualified. The SAT I's claim to be the "gold standard of quality" derives from its purported ability to predict how students will perform in their first year of college. Of the various tests that make up the SAT I aptitude and the SAT II achievement tests, the best single predictor of student performance turned out to be the SAT II writing test. This test is the only one of the group that requires students to write something in addition to answering multiple-choice items. Given the importance of writing ability at the college level, it should not be surprising that a test of actual writing skills correlates strongly with freshman grades.

Curriculum-based Tests

We should use standardized tests that have a demonstrable relationship to the specific subjects taught in high schools. This would benefit students, because much time is currently wasted inside and outside the classroom prepping students for the SAT I; the time could be better spent learning history or geometry.

Appropriate Role of Standardized Tests

Finally, I have argued that U.S. universities should employ admissions processes that look at individual applicants broadly and take special pains to ensure that standardized tests are used properly in admissions decisions. To do this, we must assess students in their full complexity. This means considering not only grades and test scores but also what students have made of their opportunities to learn, the obstacles they have overcome, and the special talents they possess.

Achievement tests are fairer to students because they measure accomplishment rather than ill-defined notions of aptitude; they can be used to improve performance; they are less vulnerable

Relationship between student's family income and SAT scores (by subject), 2009

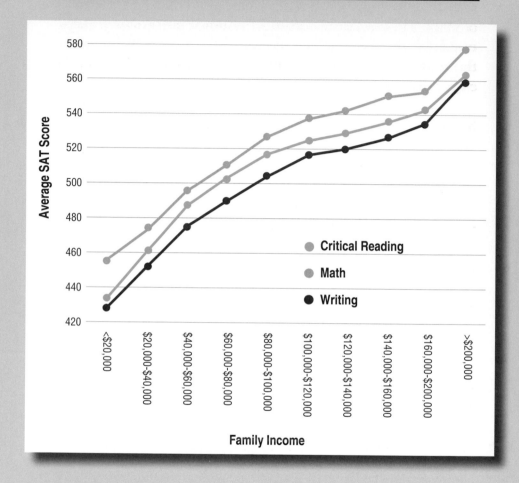

Average SAT Score

● Critical Reading

● Math

● Writing

Family Income

Source: College Board

to charges of cultural or socioeconomic bias; and they are more appropriate for schools, because they set clear curricular guidelines and clarify what is important for students to learn. Most important, they tell students that a college education is within the reach of anyone with the talent and determination to succeed.

For all of these reasons, the movement away from aptitude tests toward achievement tests is an appropriate step for U.S.

students, schools, and universities. Our goal in setting admissions requirements should be to reward excellence in all its forms and to minimize, to the greatest extent possible, the barriers students face in realizing their potential. We intend to honor both the ideal of merit and the ideal of broad educational opportunity. These twin ideals are deeply woven into the fabric of higher education in this country. It is no exaggeration to say that they are the defining characteristics of the U.S. system of higher education.

The irony of the SAT I is that it began as an effort to move higher education closer to egalitarian values. Yet its roots are in a very different tradition: the IQ testing that took place during the First World War, when two million men were tested and assigned an IQ based on the results. The framers of these tests assumed that intelligence was a unitary inherited attribute, that it was not subject to change over a lifetime, and that it could be measured and individuals could be ranked and assigned their place in society accordingly. Although the SAT I is more sophisticated from a psychometric standpoint, it evolved from the same questionable assumptions about human talent and potential.

The tests we use to judge our students influence many lives, sometimes profoundly. We need a national discussion on standardized testing, informed by principle and disciplined by empirical evidence. We will never devise the perfect test: a test that accurately assesses students irrespective of parental education and income, the quality of local schools, and the kind of community students live in. But we can do better. We can do much better.

SIX

The Rich-Poor Divide on College Campuses Is Widening

Jon Marcus and Holly K. Hacker

In the following excerpted viewpoint, Jon Marcus and Holly K. Hacker argue that college used to be a way for students from lower economic environments to achieve a better standard of living. However, they feel that today's college admissions processes are making the divide between rich and poor even greater. Lower income students who can't afford expensive colleges or college prep strategies are forced to attend schools where their chances of success are less. Marcus is a higher-education editor who has written for the *Washington Post*, *USA Today*, *Time*, the *Boston Globe*, and *Washington Monthly* and contributed to the book *Reinventing Higher Education*. Hacker is an education reporter and data specialist at the *Dallas Morning News*.

Once acclaimed as the equal-opportunity stepping stone to the middle class, and a way of closing that divide, higher education has instead become more segregated than ever by wealth and race as state funding has fallen and colleges and universities— and even states and the federal government—are shifting financial aid from lower-income to higher-income students. This has created a system that spends the least on those who need the most help and the most on those who arguably need the least. While almost all

Economic differences can be obvious just by looking at a public, private, or community college campus.

the students who go to selective institutions such as Trinity graduate and get good jobs, many students from the poorest families end up even worse off than they started out, struggling to repay loans they took out to pay for degrees they never get.

"Something of a Caste System"

Instead of raising people up, "Today in many ways the system is exacerbating inequality," said Suzanne Mettler, a government professor at Cornell University and author of *Degrees of Inequality: Why Opportunity Has Diminished in U.S. Higher Education.* "It's creating something of a caste system that for too many people takes them from wherever they were on the socioeconomic spectrum and leaves them even more unequal."

Or, as Julian Lopez, a student catching up on his homework between classes at Capital Community College, puts it: "There are plenty of smart people here. But everything's about the money. The majority of people who come here, it's because they can't afford to go to more expensive schools. It depends on how much money you have and how much money your parents make."

Only 7 percent of students graduate from the two-year college within even three years, according to the U.S. Department of Education. (The school says another 23 percent transfer.) At Trinity, 86 percent of students finish their four-year degrees within six years.

In part because of disparities like this, students from high-income families are a staggering eight times more likely to get bachelor's degrees by the time they're 24 than from low-income families, up from six times more likely in 1970, according to the Pell Institute for the Study of Opportunity in Higher Education.

"It's Not About Academic Ability"

"The gap between the haves and the have-nots is just getting bigger," said Laura Perna, chairman of the higher-education division at the University of Pennsylvania Graduate School of Education. "Really it calls into question the American dream. We tell people, just work hard and you'll have these opportunities available. The reality is, if you grow up in a neighborhood in West Philadelphia, your chances are quite different than if you grow up just a few miles away in a family with a quite higher income."

It's not about academic ability. The lowest-income students with the highest scores on eighth-grade standardized tests are less likely to go to selective colleges than the highest-income students with the lowest test scores, according to the Education Trust, which advocates for students who are being left behind in this way. If they do manage to make it to a top school, many do well —at Trinity, for instance, finishing with even higher graduation rates than their wealthier classmates.

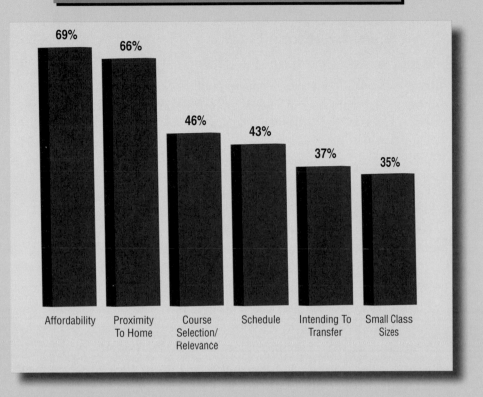

Top reasons students choose to attend community colleges

69% Affordability
66% Proximity To Home
46% Course Selection/Relevance
43% Schedule
37% Intending To Transfer
35% Small Class Sizes

Source: Cengage Learning

Another of those reasons: Students from schools in higher-income suburbs usually do better on college entrances exams such as the SAT and other measures that make the universities and colleges that accept them look better in national rankings.

"We've almost built this system that isn't set up to open its doors to low-income students," said Angel Pérez, Trinity's vice president of enrollment and student success.

Himself the son of Puerto Rican immigrants, raised in the projects of the South Bronx, Pérez said, "Admitting kids that share my story is riskier these days. Take too many and your average

GPA or SAT scores decrease. There goes your *U.S. News* ranking. Admit students who don't have the best stats and you might damage your yield and retention numbers. There goes your Moody's bond rating."

"We're on the Wrong Path"

Meanwhile, families in the top 10 percent of incomes have vastly increased what they spend on such things as test preparation, private schools, and other things meant to give their kids a leg up in admission, according to a report by the Stanford Center on Poverty and Inequality.

"High-income parents have resources they can use for this, and low-income parents have had to cut back," said Sabino Kornrich, a professor of sociology at Emory University who coauthored the report. "We've seen since the recession this inequality of spending become even more pronounced."

What students in those poorer institutions get is far inferior to what their counterparts at richer schools enjoy. The dropout rate at community colleges is higher than it is at high schools; while 81 percent of students who start in one say they eventually want to transfer and earn at least a bachelor's degree, only 12 percent of them do, the Century Foundation reports.

At Trinity, by comparison, "For me and I know for most students here, my only worry is getting my homework done, because everything else is sort of given to us," said Miguel Adamson, an international studies major, sitting under a tree on the campus working on his laptop. Members of the squash team pass by through arched passageways hung with flyers advertising an organ recital and internship and study-abroad programs, and another student outfitted in Vineyard Vines apparel stops by to say hello.

"These sorts of schools are places where you can really see the economic divide, especially between people who get a lot of financial aid and people who don't, even by what they're wearing," said Adamson, who went to private school in Washington D.C.

With relatives who are lower-income—including a cousin with whom he has discussed this issue—he has been "more exposed,

I think, to what some people are up against," Adamson said. "I would take things for granted and she would yell at me, 'You don't know what the struggles are.'"

Access to an equitable college education "is really crucial to what America is, was, and at least used to stand for," he said. "It clearly doesn't stand for that any more. The data show, in every way you look at it, that we're on the wrong path."

SEVEN

Six Ways Colleges Game Their Numbers

Marian Wang

> In the following viewpoint, Marian Wang argues that schools are inflating their statistics by making it easier for more—often unqualified—students to apply. This makes the percentage of accepted students smaller and, in turn, makes the school seem more exclusive. One of the ways colleges attract students is by offering such data to prove how exclusive and high-quality their programs are. Prospective students view statistics such as the number of applications, the rate of acceptance, and the average test score of accepted students, and those numbers may factor into their application decisions. The author contends that such skewed data is flawed and that prospective students should be aware of the admissions game. Wang is a reporter for ProPublica, covering education and college debt.

As college-bound students weigh their options, they often look to the various statistics that universities trumpet—things like the high number of applications, high test scores, and low acceptance rate.

But students may want to consider yet another piece of info: the ways in which schools can pump up their stats.

"There's no question about it," said David Kalsbeek, senior vice president for enrollment management and marketing at DePaul University. "There are ways of inflating a metric to improve perceived measures of quality."

"The Admission Arms Race: Six Ways Colleges Game Their Numbers," by Marian Wang, Pro Publica Inc., April 23, 2013. Reprinted by permission. Courtesy of ProPublica.

Colleges can misrepresent themselves to prospective students, who should learn how to interpret admissions data and ask the right questions.

Some of these tweaks—such as a more streamlined application—can actually benefit students. Others serve to make the admissions process more confusing. Here's a rundown.

1) Quickie, often pre-filled out applications

Express applications—sometimes known as "fast apps," "snap apps," "V.I.P. applications" or "priority applications"—are often pre-filled with some student information and require little if anything in the way of essays. And especially when they're accompanied with an application-fee waiver, what's a student got to lose? Not much, fans of fast apps argue.

The school, meanwhile, has a lot to gain. The tactic, designed to broaden the pool of applicants, can help super-charge application numbers. Drexel University and St. John's University—the only two private colleges among the top 10 for most applied-to colleges in 2011—both market broadly and use fast apps.

Both schools received roughly 50,000 applications in the fall of 2011, according to U.S. News data. Both schools enroll roughly 3,000 freshmen.

Getting in more applications can also boost the appearance of selectivity. Critics contend that some schools use fast apps specifically for this purpose—luring students in to apply to institutions they hadn't heard of and ultimately rejecting a portion of them. Neither school, when contacted, responded to requests for comment.

2) Shorter applications, Common Applications, and shorter Common Applications

Another way to get more applications is to adopt the Common Application, as nearly 500 colleges have since its inception in 1975. The form, which lets students apply to multiple schools at once, has fueled the long-term rise in applications. And as more colleges have adopted it, other schools have felt pressure to start using it too.

Many schools have long required that students submitting a Common Application include additional answers or essays. Dropping the extra requirements can result in a spike in applications. That's what happened for Skidmore College, which saw a 42 percent jump in applications this cycle after it stopped requiring supplemental essays to the Common App. (Skidmore College's dean of admissions did not respond to a request for an interview.)

3) Dipping into early application pools

Another statistic schools often try to control is their "yield"— that's admissions parlance for the percentage of students offered admission that choose to attend.

Though it's no longer statistically factored into *U.S. News & World Report*'s ubiquitous rankings, yield rates are still a data point made available to prospective students. They're also inextricably

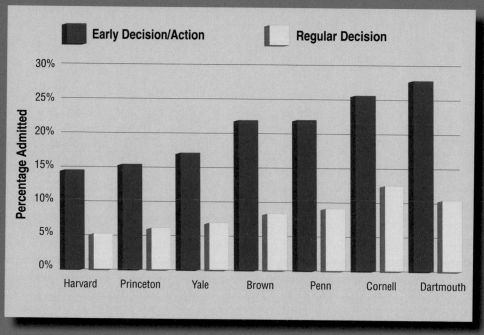

Early decision/action acceptance rates versus regular decision acceptance rates at Ivy League universities, class of 2021

■ Early Decision/Action □ Regular Decision

Percentage Admitted

| | Harvard | Princeton | Yale | Brown | Penn | Cornell | Dartmouth |

Sources: IvyWise and Business Insider

tied to acceptance rates because schools use previous yields to calculate how many students they should admit to fill a class. Schools with low yields must extend lots of acceptances, knowing many accepted students will go elsewhere.

One way to increase yields is to draw heavily from the pool of applicants who chose to apply through early action, or to encourage early decision, which is binding. At the University of Pennsylvania, for instance, nearly half of the spots in the freshman class are filled through the university's binding early decision process.

Penn is hardly alone in leaning heavily on early decision. Many schools accept early decision applicants at a higher rate than students who apply later. American University, for instance, accepts about 75 percent of early decision applicants, though its overall acceptance rate is far lower.

One other thing to note: Because early decision involves committing before any financial aid is offered, it generally attracts wealthier families. Students who need financial aid or want to be able to make cost comparisons between different schools are typically advised not to apply early—which can hurt their chances.

4) Rejecting good students universities think are just using them as a backup

While opening up early decision and early action programs is a way for colleges to force students to demonstrate that they're their top choice, schools use a variety of ways to divine the same information from regular decision students as well. This is perhaps the most common—and in some ways, common sense—method used by colleges to improve yield: simply to admit only those students who they perceive as likely to enroll.

"There are so many silent electronic footprints they're leaving nowadays," said Sundar Kumarasamy, vice president for enrollment management and marketing at the University of Dayton.

Kumarasamy said that his institution tracks many of these subtle signals of interest from applicants: They can tell whether individual applicants clicked to open email communications, logged into the system to check the status of an application, and not only whether they called the school, but how long that phone call lasted. If the school gets the sense that an applicant isn't interested, that's factored in. Kumarasamy calls it "recruiting for fit."

The interest—or lack thereof—can ultimately mean that the school rejects some candidates who on paper are more than qualified but failed to demonstrate interest.

5) Making tests optional

One admissions trend within the past decade has been the test-optional movement. Colleges that have stopped requiring standardized test scores often cite equity and diversity as reasons to make the move, noting the strong correlation between socio-economic status and test scores.

But going test-optional can also help universities' stats. Critics note that in addition to attracting more applicants, the move ultimately skews the average test scores that institutions report: Lower-scoring applicants are the most likely to withhold their scores and higher-scoring applicants are the most likely to submit them.

6) Making stuff up

Some colleges actually cross the line with their creative number crunching. Since the start of last year, five colleges have acknowledged overstating their admissions statistics: Bucknell University, Claremont McKenna College, Emory University, George Washington University, and Tulane University's business school.

Admissions data is self-reported and no outside party is responsible for verifying it. The recent scandals involving falsified data have only come to light after colleges disclosed the problems themselves.

U.S. News' Robert Morse has said there is "no reason to believe that the misreporting is widespread." But a survey by Inside Higher Ed last fall suggests that even admissions directors are skeptical of the reporting, with 91 percent of those surveyed saying believe they believe there's more misreporting than has been identified.

Of course, some colleges resist the pressure to pump up admissions numbers. Doing so is unusual enough that it attracts notice and media write-ups.

Boston College made "a strategic decision" this cycle to raise the admissions bar by adding an essay. It got the expected drop in applications—and a recent write-up in the *New York Times*. A handful of others, including Ursinus College, have done the same. In addition to requiring essays again, they dropped the fast app.

But for many other colleges, what's been called the admissions "arms race" is on—with these strategically achieved statistics as the scoreboard.

Students Need Quality College Counseling

Robert Bardwell

> In the following viewpoint, Robert Bardwell argues that it is not enough to encourage more students to attend higher education institutions, even if tuitions are lowered or funding is available. College admissions is an increasingly tricky business, and most students need guidance in navigating the application and financial aid process. Yet, as the author contends, there are not enough school guidance counselors in most high schools to help students successfully identify and apply to colleges. He offers some possible solutions for this problem, including what noncounselors can do to assist students in making their choices. Bardwell is a school counselor and director of guidance and student support services at Monson High School in Monson, Massachusetts.

President Obama said these words during his 2009 State of the Union address:

> *Tonight, I ask every American to commit to at least one year or more of higher education or career training. This can be community college or a four-year school; vocational training or an apprenticeship. But whatever the training may be, every American will need to get more than a high school diploma ... That is why we will provide the support necessary for you to complete college and meet a new goal: by 2020, America will once again have the highest proportion of college graduates in the world.*

"Improving College Counseling," by Robert Bardwell, ASCD, April 2012. Reprinted by permission.

The college admissions process is an increasingly complicated and confusing undertaking. Students can benefit from the expertise of a counselor.

K–12 educators and higher education officials were ecstatic to hear a president talking their talk. President Obama didn't just give facile praise to the 3.29 million U.S. students who head off to college every year (*Chronicle of Higher Education*, 2008)—he raised the bar to encourage more citizens to further their education.

It's heartening to hear the president support universal post-secondary education so forcefully. But do we have the supports in place to achieve this goal? Specifically, do U.S. schools have enough counselors so that all students can explore college or career training? Navigating the college application process and finding money for tuition are tricky; most students need help. Within schools, counselors are the single most important professionals in terms of improving students' college-going rates (McDonough, 2006). Yet many schools simply don't have enough school counselors to help students with postsecondary plans.

In 2010, the average student-to-school counselor ratio in the United States was 459 to 1; the American School Counselor Association (n.d.) recommends a ratio of 250 to 1. At schools with high student-to-counselor ratios, advising is more limited and is often reactive rather than proactive (Perna et al., 2008).

Compounding the problem is the fact that most counselors have a limited amount of time for college-counseling activities. According to the National Association for College Admission Couseling (NACAC, 2008), high school counselors spend, on average, 29 percent of their time on college counseling (23 percent in public schools and 58 percent in private schools). Even in schools that have a decent student-to-counselor ratio, counselors are consumed by such activities as test administration, substitute coverage, or paperwork. This is especially a problem in terms of guiding low-income students because the school counselor is often the only adult to provide them such information (Cabrera & LaNasa, 2000). In more affluent communities, counselors generally have more time, and most private schools have counselors whose only job is college advising (NACAC, 2008). Ironically, the students who need help most get the least.

Even when a school has enough professionals with the time to give most students guidance on postsecondary plans, willing counselors may not be able to provide well-informed help. Many school counselors don't receive adequate preparation in the area of college-admission counseling. In 2004, only 66 percent of school counselors reported that they had received any kind of training in how to help with the college search and application process during the past year (NACAC, 2004). Only 24 percent said they had taken graduate coursework in this area.

Nor do things look better from the students' point of view: A 2010 study by Public Agenda found that 48 percent of young adults surveyed believed that their school counselor was of little

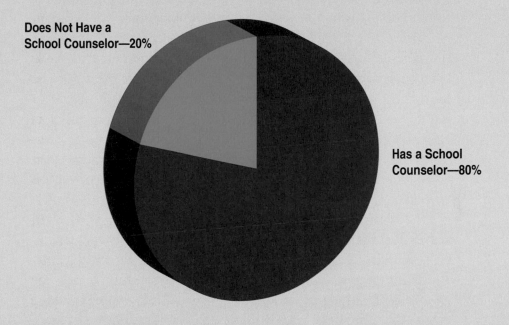

Percentage of high schools nationwide with and without school counselors, 2014

Does Not Have a
School Counselor—20%

Has a School
Counselor—80%

Source: U.S. Department of Education Office for Civil Rights

to no assistance in their college search. They felt their counselor treated them like another face in the crowd (Johnson, Rochkind, Ott, & DuPont, 2010).

On the positive side, school counselors and administrators care about helping youth set college as a goal and attaining it. There are things that administrators and school counselors can do to improve the college-going culture in their schools, despite a lack of resources. But we'll need to try different approaches.

Invite the Village to Explore

The phrase "it takes a village" is certainly true when it comes to supporting students' pursuit of higher education. Parents, students, teachers, administrators, business community members, and higher education officials must cooperate in developing an action plan. They must together identify local resource gaps or barriers to higher education—and compose a plan to create solutions.

Working together through existing advisory groups or a new committee, these stakeholders should examine college-going rates of different schools or communities in their area, looking for patterns. To identify which existing programs do or don't work, they should survey community youth. Which students have been most successful and persistent? What helped them? Why did certain groups of students choose not to pursue college? What might have been done differently in middle and early high school to change their minds?

School counselors should lead such efforts at least once a year to ensure that administrators, parents, and business partners use current information as they design and implement programs.

Crunch Data

Sometimes studying data is the last thing school counselors want to do. I've heard school personnel say, "I didn't go into this profession to crunch numbers. I want to help students." But if we care about getting kids to college, we can no longer avoid collecting, analyzing, and reporting key data points that affect students' ability to gain access to education.

To better support all students' pursuit of college or high-quality career training, counselors and administrators should look at course enrollment patterns. Is a representative sample of students taking courses needed to pursue postsecondary education? Are girls and students of color enrolling in math courses? Do all students have the opportunity to learn a foreign language?

Math and English faculty and counselors might together review students' results from college admissions tests. They may see, through item analysis, areas in which the existing curriculum supported success and areas in which students struggled on standardized tests. To close the gaps, teachers can then introduce new topics into the curriculum. It's also good to examine data on graduates of the areas' schools, including which colleges accepted students with various qualifications. Counselors and teachers can then sketch the profile of a typical successful applicant for each college.

Launch Innovative Programs

It's essential to get into the hands of students and families information on how to select and apply to colleges. Sometimes we have to do this more than once through attention-grabbing formats. Consider sponsoring a career-and-college-awareness week at middle and high schools, filled with activities like these to expose students to new information:

- Field trips to local or regional college fairs.
- Evening programs for parents about the basics of the college application and admission process.
- Speakers who cover such topics as writing a great college essay, understanding financial aid, or completing the Common Application online.

Some schools conduct a friendly competition centered on postsecondary options, for example, the best door display highlighting a college or career. A display could include information about costs for the nearby state university, demographics for typical attendees, and a list of its strongest majors and activities. Bring in celebrity judges, such as noted alumni, district administrators, or community business leaders. Create opportunities for all students to explore the information showcased through the contest.

Another way to get attention is to bring recent alumni back to speak to students about their college experiences. Try January programs for freshmen and sophomores and a May program for seniors focused on surviving the stress of the transition into college.

Start Early

Changing a school's culture to promote pursuit of postsecondary education should be a K–12 responsibility. Counselors can deliver developmentally appropriate lessons at any grade level on such topics as how to set career goals; different types of colleges (such as community versus four-year, private versus public); and the relationship between education attainment and income. These efforts will communicate early on the expectation that all students must be career- and college-ready by high school graduation.

Besides traditional lessons, try providing activities like these:

- A career or college fair for elementary and middle school students.

- Exploratory and hands-on programs that showcase a particular career cluster.

- A College Pride day for which faculty wear a sweatshirt or other fashion item from their alma mater.

Reach Out to Underserved Groups

Some groups, such as students with learning disabilities, first-generation college goers, English language learners, and undocumented students or families, will need targeted programs that deliver information and encouragement about postsecondary options in a clear and convincing way. Schools might

- Host a potluck dinner for first-generation college-going students and their parents that includes presentations—in families' native languages when possible—on the college application process. Emphasize the importance of college in a fun way, such as by creating a trivia game of facts about local colleges or aspects of the college application process for the group to play.

- Partner with community groups to translate programs and materials for ethnic groups.

- Ask students who have either successfully completed college or are currently in a postsecondary program to mentor youth who need extra attention.

President Obama's admirable goal will never be achieved without significant changes in how we deliver career and college counseling services. Schools must get past the idea that only counselors, using traditional one-on-one visits, can point students toward postsecondary options. Let's keep our focus on doing more with less so we can guide all students, and guide those who want to go into college successfully down that route. There's too much at stake not to.

References

American School Counselor Association. (n.d.). *Student-to-school-counselor-ratios*. Alexandria, VA: Author. Retrieved from www.schoolcounselor.org/content.asp?pl=655&contentid=655).

Chronicle of Higher Education. (2008) *Almanac Issue, 55*(1).

Cabrera, A. F., & LaNasa, S. M. (2000). Understanding the college process. *New Directions for Institutional Research, 107*, 5–22.

Johnson, J., Rochkind, J. Ott, A. N., & DuPont, S. (2010). *Can I get a little advice here?* New York: Public Agenda.

McDonough, P. (2006). Counseling and college counseling in America's schools. In *Fundamentals of College Admission Counseling* (2nd ed., pp. 2–21). Alexandria, VA: NACAC.

NACAC. (2004) *State of college admission report*. Alexandria, VA: Author.

NACAC. (2008). *State of college admission report*. Alexandria, VA: NACAC.

National Center for Education Statistics. (2003). *High school guidance counseling*. Washington, DC: Author. Retrieved from http://nces.ed.gov/pubs2003/2003015.pdf.

Perna, L. W., Rowan-Kenyon, H. T., Thomas, S., Bell, A., Anderson, R., & Li, C., (2008). The role of college counseling in shaping college opportunities: Variations across high schools. *The Review of Higher Education, 31*(2), 131–159.

NINE

How Can the College Application Process Be Improved?

Holly Korbey

In the following viewpoint, Holly Korbey argues that the college admissions process could be improved by shifting priorities and timelines. Korbey points out that the college application process has become too stressful and also forces students to focus on personal success and not on contributions to the community. This also puts low-income students at a disadvantage. She sets out some specific suggestions for improving the process with new tools and methods, such as beginning the process in middle school to help students focus and gradually work to their goal. Korbey is a journalist whose work on parenting and education has appeared in the *New York Times*, the *Atlantic*, *Babble*, *Brain*, *Child Magazine*, and other publications.

Over the last few years, voices from various arenas have begun to complain that increased competition in the college admissions process has become too stressful, too focused on getting into the "right" college, and overly focused on personal success.

A recent report by Harvard's Making Caring Common, called "Turning the Tide," was written after it conducted a survey of 10,000 middle and high school students and found that only 22 percent ranked "caring for others" as more important than their

"How Can the College Application Process Be Improved?" by Holly Korbey, KQED, March 7, 2016. Reprinted by permission.

The byzantine college application process can have negative effects on both students and universities.

own personal success and happiness.[1] The report pleads for a kinder, gentler college admissions process that would deemphasize the importance of classic academic markers like AP classes and test scores, and asks to make sure students provide proof that community service projects had real meaning in their lives.

But more importantly, it calls out ways in which the top-tier colleges "shut out" lower-income students through tactics like legacy admissions and early-decision applications.[2] Frank Bruni, writing in the *New York Times*, articulates how the overly competitive admissions process "warps the values of students drawn into a competitive frenzy. It jeopardizes their mental health. And it fails to include—and identify the potential in—enough kids from less privileged backgrounds."[3]

The competition to get into the nation's top colleges has been on the rise, some of it simply the result of more eligible students, both here and from around the world. "The increase in students and applications continue to push acceptance rates lower and lower," wrote Lindsey Cook, data editor for *U.S. News and World Report*, in a piece about the stress and competition wrapped around college admissions. "In 1988, the acceptance rate for Columbia University in New York was 65 percent, according to *U.S. News & World Report*'s Best Colleges edition that year. In our most recent guide, 33,531 applied to Columbia and 2,311 were accepted. That's not even 7 percent."[4]

"For the last thirty years the machinery of college admissions has solved the administrative problem created by America's surfeit of smart and eager high-school students," laments Matt Feeney in his recent *New Yorker* piece, "by inventing new, pedagogically empty ways for them to compete with one another, laying out new grounds on which they might fight one another."[5]

Universities, as well as some organizations, are looking at how students apply to college and asking what can be done to revamp and renew the process and make it more equitable, raising some sincere questions: Is it the applications process itself that's unfair? If applying to college could start earlier, would that lessen the stress and even the playing field, and make the nation's top colleges accessible to different kinds of students? Or would it just increase the pressure?

Early Conversations

Veronica Hauad still has the paper file folder given to her by her high school admissions counselor early in her high school career. Following her counselor's direction, over four years, Hauad slowly filled it with everything she wanted to have on hand when she applied to college: her transcripts, test scores, awards she won, the now-obsolete floppy disk of her college essay.

Now the deputy dean of admissions and director of Equity and Access Programming at the University of Chicago, Hauad keeps the overflowing folder in her office, to remind both herself and

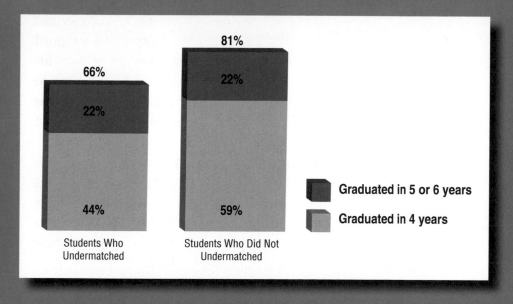

College graduation rate of students who undermatched compared to those who did not

66%

22%

44%

Students Who
Undermatched

81%

22%

59%

Students Who Did Not
Undermatched

■ Graduated in 5 or 6 years

□ Graduated in 4 years

Source: William G. Bowen, Matthew Chingos, and Michael S. McPherson, Crossing the Finish Line: Completing College at America's Public Universities

high school applicants that "the application process shouldn't be this frenzied process in the fall of your senior year, which is already busy," she said. "Let's think long term, about my identity and what my application will look like."

It's also there to remind Hauad how technology has changed college admissions.

The University of Chicago is one of more than 80 top-tier colleges and universities that joined together to form the Coalition for Access, Affordability and Success this past fall, with the mission of improving the college application process for all students.[6] Schools that have joined the coalition—including all the Ivy League schools, more than 30 public and research universities as well as small liberal arts colleges—must meet certain requirements, including a high graduation rate[7] and meeting a large portion of demonstrated financial need or offering low in-state tuition.

The coalition's approach will have three key components:

- The application itself, which will debut in July and will be similar to most other online college applications

- A digital locker, or online storage, available in April 2016, where students can store work they may like to include in their college application beginning in ninth grade, including written work as well as audio and video of performances or exhibitions

- A collaboration platform (also coming in April) that allows students to share their application and essay with a coach or mentor to receive feedback and advice before submitting.

The coalition promises its platform will be smoother and more reliable than the more universal Common App, used to apply to more than 600 schools, which has been plagued with technical issues in the past.[8] (The Common App, in what may be a response to the coalition's platform, has also beefed up its website to include a rollover application students can fill out beginning junior year, a platform for school counselors to guide students through the process, and a free mobile app, Common App on Track, which will help remind students of upcoming application deadlines.)[9]

While the coalition's new application and collaboration platform promise to make the application process smoother and easier, exactly how the its free site will give lower-income students better access and equality to top-tier schools is a little less clear, except maybe to give students more information on schools they may not have heard of or assumed were out of their league academically or financially.

Hauad said that even though the coalition application will be the same, how schools evaluate applications varies in every case. "There are colleges that don't require testing, some do. There are colleges that don't really rely on recommendations, some do," she said. "So we're all doing this different ways as it currently stands."

Hauad said the coalition hopes that the impressive list of schools, coupled with the free application tools, will get students thinking that their chances of going to a more highly selective (and more expensive) school might be better than they think. Hauad said what she loves about the coalition app is that an underrepresented student may look at the list and recognize some names, but then also see some colleges she's never heard of.

"I think part of the frenzy of college admissions in this country is the idea that there are only 12–15 schools worth going to, and that is not true," she said. "There are tons of schools serving students with tons of amazing ways, in and out of the classroom, financially, and post-grad. I love that you can look at this list and say, here are some schools that I recognize, here are some other schools that are keeping company with these great schools, now I fleshed out a bigger list."

Many coalition schools waive application fees if a student is applying for financial aid, making it easy for lower-income students to apply to more schools. And from the coalition's point of view, a bigger list is an ideal list.

Schools are Getting Ready

High school guidance counselor Joe Levickis oversees 113 seniors, along with about 200 more freshmen, sophomores and juniors, at Hunter's Lane High School, located on the northern tip of Nashville, Tennessee. When he's asked when he starts talking to his students—86 percent of whom live below the poverty line—about college, Levickis, 26 and a first-generation college graduate himself, smiles.

"The day they walk in the door," he said.

Hunter's Lane has about 1,700 students divided into smaller and more personal 350-student academies, where counselors like Levickis get to spend four years with the same kids, all of whom are on a college-prep track. Beginning with a seminar class at the start of freshman year, Levickis and the team of teachers are talking to the students about college—on-campus college fairs, visits to surrounding schools and even college-shirt day—from the day they start high school.

Since many of their students will be first in their families to apply to college, anything they can do to help their students get serious about college they consider a good thing. To that end, all the college prep appears to be paying off at first glance: 75 percent of the Hunter's Lane graduating class of 2015 got into the two- or four-year college of their choice, and together the students earned over $5 million in scholarships, which is a huge win for both the students and the school.

Levickis said the top four schools where his students were accepted were Nashville State Community College, Volunteer State Community College, Tennessee State University and Austin Peay, all schools less than 50 miles from Nashville. Levickis said he didn't know of any Hunter's Lane students who applied to Ivy League schools last year, though one student who is graduating in 2016 did a recent interview at the Citadel.

Both Levickis and principal Dr. Susan Kessler got excited about the coalition's idea of the digital locker, and beginning to have students gather and store their work beginning in ninth grade, which supports all the work they do getting their kids to plan to go to college. They also think that an easy and free way to apply to the bigger schools might encourage students to shoot for the stars.

But Dr. Susan Kessler admits that getting her students *into* college isn't really the problem, it's getting the students to show up on the first day. While Hunter's Lane tracks where each student gets into college, it has no idea how many kids show up to those colleges in the fall, but knows that it's not anywhere near the 75 percent.

Because so many students live on the edge of poverty, actually attending the college that accepted them means all of their stars must align by August: one illness, broken-down car or unexpected expense like the cost of books might mean that students who worked so hard to apply and get into college never show up for their first class.

Kessler tells the story of when she took her own son to college, and realized once they got there that he needed more stuff:

"I had to go to the local Wal-Mart and spent $700. Well, I live in a two-income family, and I can have an unexpected expense like that," she said. "But if you're living at the poverty level, then you can't. So things like that, or an illness in the family, a parental illness, that stuff often gets in the way of children going off to school."

Even so, Levickis and Kessler say that any tool, especially a free one, that will make it easier for their students to apply to college is a useful one, even though the coalition's effort to reach students like the ones at Hunter's Lane calls into question whether a new kind of application will actually help the students it's trying to reach, who often have much more basic problems.

Hauad emphasizes that the coalition's new tools may not solve all the problems with elite college admissions, but are nonetheless an important first step.

"I'm really excited about the potential here and I think it's something people forget," Hauad said. "No one's saying that it's The Answer, capital A, to any one thing. But I'm excited about the potential. And to me, potential is where you can make a difference in a lot of ways. So I'm very excited, as a practitioner working in access, about the potential."

Notes

1. Making Caring Common Project, Harvard Graduate School of Education, "Turning the Tide." http://mcc.gse.harvard.edu/files/gse-mcc/files/20160120 _mcc_ttt_execsummary_interactive.pdf?m=1453303460

2. Kamenetz, Anya, "5 Ways Elite-College Admissions Shut Out Poor Kids," npr, January 15, 2016. http://www.npr.org/sections /ed/2016/01/15/462149341/5-ways-elite-college-admissions-squeeze-out-poor-kids?utm_source=facebook.com&utm_medium=social&utm_campaign=n-pr&utm_term=nprnews&utm_content=20160115

3. Bruni, Frank, "Rethinking College Admissions," The New York Times, January 19, 2016. https://www.nytimes.com/2016/01/20/opinion /rethinking-college-admissions.html?smid=fb-share&_r=0

4. Cook, Lindsey, "Is the College Admissions Bubble About to Burst?" US News and World Report, September 22, 2014. https://www.usnews.com/news /blogs/data-mine/2014/09/22/is-the-college-admissions-bubble-about-to-burst

5. Feeney, Matt, "The Poisonous Reach of the College-Admissions Process," The New Yorker, January 28, 2016. http://www.newyorker.com/culture

/cultural-comment/the-poisonous-reach-of-the-college-admissions-process
?mbid=social_facebook

6. Coalition for Access, Affordability, and Success. http://www
.coalitionforcollegeaccess.org/

7. Westervelt, Eric, "The Big New Effort to Revamp College Admissions—
Will it Work?" npr, September 30, 2015. http://www.npr.org/sections
/ed/2015/09/30/444498625
/the-big-new-effort-to-revamp-college-admissions-will-it-work

8. Boyington, Briana, "How to Handle Complications with the Common
App," US News and World Report, December 18, 2013. https://www.usnews
.com/education/best-colleges/articles/2013/12/18
/how-to-handle-complications-with-the-common-app

9. The Common Application, November 30, 2015. http://www.commonapp
.org/whats-appening/news
/common-application-launches-its-first-mobile-app-common-app-ontrack-0

TEN

Think Twice Before Paying for College Prep Professionals

Caralee J. Adams

> In the following viewpoint, Caralee J. Adams discusses the trend toward expensive test prep and college admissions courses and tutors, which are supposed to help students get into the colleges of their choice. She also discusses whether these test prep systems are worthwhile and how students can achieve similar results on their own. As applying for college has become more complicated, an entire industry has sprung up to help—and capitalize on—students desperate to get into the school of their choice. Adams is a contributing writer for *Education Week* specializing in higher education. She is also author of the blog College Bound.

The anxiety of high school juniors—and their parents—over taking college-entrance exams is creating a market force for the test-preparation industry.

Dozens of companies are flooding mailboxes with offers to hire tutors and enroll in classes, including online courses to make preparation for the high-stakes tests more convenient and customized.

Those in the business claim students will improve their performance, and many offer money-back guarantees. Yet outside research shows coaching has minimal positive effects, although there hasn't been a randomized, controlled experiment to isolate the impact of test prep.

"Value of College-Admissions Test-Prep Classes Unclear," by Caralee J. Adams, Editorial Projects in Education, February 24, 2011. Reprinted by permission.

Despite pressure to hire tutors and enroll in expensive test prep classes, there are plenty of cheap alternatives for motivated students.

No federal agency has stepped in to provide industry oversight, so experts suggest that consumers do their homework before shelling out money and make sure the prep service is the right fit for their child. For some students, one-on-one tutoring is the most cost-effective; others do best in a classroom. And for many, a $25 test-prep book or free online tests is all they need.

"Parents are sacrificing, even borrowing on their credit cards to pay these high prices for prep courses," said Dave Berry, a co-founder of and senior adviser for College Confidential, a college-admissions website. "In fact, kids—if they are dedicated, that's a big if—can get the prep books and do the exercises and most likely increase their scores to within a reasonable degree of the amount they could get through the prep courses."

No matter what a student chooses, counselors caution that students keep in mind test scores are just one part of the college-admissions decision. According to surveys by the National Association for College Admission Counselors, in Arlington, Va., SAT and ACT scores have consistently ranked third in importance, behind grades and strength of curriculum.

"High SATs do not get you into college, a strong academic record does," said Debra Shaver, the director of admissions at Smith College in Northampton, Mass. "Students should concentrate more on their homework and worry less about SATs."

Lack of Evidence

Derek Briggs, the chairman of the research and evaluation methodology program in the school of education at the University of Colorado at Boulder, has examined how much SAT score increases can be attributed to the effect of test prep.

Test-prep programs generally include three elements: a review of test content, practice on test questions, and orientation to the format of the test. In 2009, in cooperation with NACAC, Mr. Briggs reviewed three national data sets and found the average effect of commercial coaching is positive, but slight. Test-score bumps were more in the neighborhood of 30 points (on a 1,600-point scale at the time), far from what some in the industry claim. He does point out that there may be specific programs that are more effective than others, but evidence to support that is weak.

Considering the results of Mr. Briggs' and earlier studies, NACAC concludes that test-prep activities and coaching have a "minimal positive effect on both the SAT and the ACT."

Mr. Briggs noted that to some selective colleges, 30 points matter among high-scorers. Admissions officers are "naturally drawn to a number," and it can be one of the first filters in the process, he said. However, the New York City-based College Board, which sponsors the SAT, cautions institutions about making

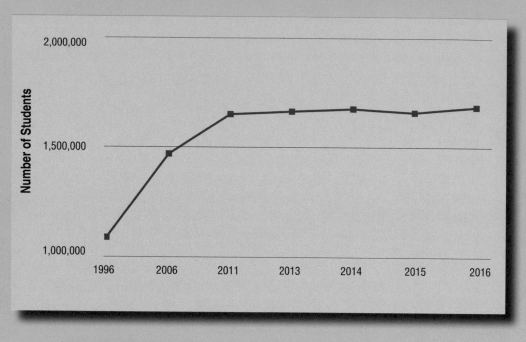

Number of students that take the SAT, by year

Source: College Board

admissions decisions about otherwise qualified students based only on small differences in test scores.

A 2006 review of 10 online websites providing SAT test-prep services by *Consumer Reports* revealed that 11th graders who used the sites saw their scores improve by an average of 38 points or a 1.6 percent gain.

Promises and Approaches

Some companies have backed off specific marketing claims. Last May, The Princeton Review, based in New York City, announced it would stop using claims about average test scores in its marketing materials. Kaplan Test Prep has ended its use of testimonials in which test-takers talk about their large score gains.

"In many ways, [claims are] misleading," said Kristen Campbell, the executive director of college-prep programs at Kaplan, also in New York City. "Instead of throwing up wild claims of points, we tell students we are committed to getting a high score." Since 2002, her company has offered students their money back or the chance to take the class again if their scores do not improve after taking the course. For competitive reasons, Kaplan won't release the number that take up on the offer other than to say the percentage is low.

Others promise specific point gains and take to task research that disputes the impact of test preparation.

Jake Neuberg and Ramit Varma, who founded Revolution Prep in California eight years ago, said research doesn't differentiate test-prep methods. With their approach of covering content, as well as managing test anxiety and increasing student motivation, they promise a 200-point gain on the SAT. Students who don't improve that much can sign up again for free. About 4.5 percent of students repeat the course because their scores did not go up by the guarantee or they had a scheduling conflict, Mr. Varma said.

Although services range from $300 to $900, Revolution doesn't turn away low-income students who can't pay. About 10 percent of students participate on scholarship.

In Bethesda, Md., Arvin Vohra founded a company and created an approach he calls the "The Vohra Method" in which students' needs are targeted and addressed in intensive seminars. He guarantees that if, after 24 weeks of training at four hours a week (at $25 per hour), the student's SAT score improves by less than 380 points, and the score is less than 2,250—out of a total of 2,400—the student can take eight more weeks for free. For those who complete the full training, nearly 100 percent meet the 380-point gain, he said.

Postcards from StudyPoint, a Boston-based company that offers in-home tutoring for $70 to $140 in several cities, advertise 200-point SAT gains. Co-founder Richard Enos says the average increase is 171 points, based on comparisons of actual SAT or PSAT tests. "Part of what programs provide is the structure, accountability, and feedback that keep students engaged and motivated," he said.

As an alternative to high-priced test prep, Number2.com is a free online service where students can take practice tests, get tailored feedback, and find tutorials for each section of the test. Launched in 1999 and sold in 2002 to Xap Corp., the site is an attempt to remove the price barrier, said co-founder Eric Loken, a professor who teaches research methodology at Pennsylvania State University.

His advice to students: "Don't buy the hype. Too often, people assume because something costs $500, it must be worth it." Many test-prep classes involve a series of practice tests that students can take at home for free, he said.

Rigorous School Courses

Test-prep courses serve a purpose, but more important is the rigor of the classes students take and practicing the test, said Steve Schneider, a counselor at Sheboygan South High School, in Sheboygan, Wis., and the American School Counselor Association's secondary-level vice president.

"I never tell a family they shouldn't do it," he said. "For some, it's not an issue to drop a couple hundred dollars. But there are more economical and impactful ways to improve your score."

The best preparation for college-admissions tests is good math and English classes in high school, said Lisa Sohmer, the director of college counseling at the Garden School in Jackson Heights, N.Y. "Students get from these [prep] classes precisely what they put into them," she said. "They are not a cure-all. They are simply a tool."

John Boshoven, a counselor in the Ann Arbor public schools in Ann Arbor, Mich., where everyone takes the ACT during the school day, encourages students to take the test once first to see where they need improvement. His school offers free after-school sample tests and others study on their own. "In the Midwest, we don't have the test mania or college mania as in other parts of the country," said Mr. Boshoven.

Michigan is one of about a dozen states that offer the ACT or SAT for free to all juniors, and many include free test prep.

Davis Nguyen, 18, a first-generation American from Hampton, Ga., said his Vietnamese family didn't have the money for a test-prep course. So he made a chart and studied daily for 120 hours total for the SAT. He improved his score by 300 points from one sitting to the next. Mr. Nguyen said he paced himself like a marathon runner and had to keep with the training. "For my future, I had to stay motivated," he said.

No Shortcuts

The SAT is designed to measure the academic skills students learn throughout high school and their ability to apply that knowledge, said Angela Maria Garcia, the executive director of SAT publications and information at the College Board. "The best way to get ready is to do well in school, take challenging courses, and read," she said. "There really is no short-cut to prepare for the SAT."

The College Board encourages students to use the free resources on its website, such as the SAT question of the day and practice tests to get familiar with the format.

Students often improve their score by merely taking the test a second time, as they gain more knowledge in school and are more comfortable with its structure. Colleges then take the best mix of scores from each sitting.

The Iowa City, Iowa-based ACT Inc. has developed a software program and a more extensive booklet for review, but they're really not essential, said Jon Erickson, the senior vice president for education services. "We have always been a little bit offended by test prep," he said. "It's seen as a last-ditch effort and doesn't have much effect."

Others disagree, such as Robert Schaeffer, the public education director for Jamaica Plain, Mass.-based National Center for Fair and Open Testing, or FairTest, which advocates colleges make admission tests optional. "If test-coaching didn't work, it would be the only human endeavor you can't improve," said Mr. Schaeffer. While companies may exaggerate the claims to enhance their economic self-interest, test-makers also underestimate commercial test prep to protect their product, he said.

Keeping Perspective

Test scores matter more than colleges want to admit, yet they don't trump transcripts, and parents and students need to keep perspective, said Pamela Horne, the assistant vice president for enrollment management and the dean of admissions at Purdue University in West Lafayette, Ind.

"There are companies who are in the business of ensuring that students are anxious and motivated to think this is life and death, as opposed to the idea that in the U.S. there is a place at the table of higher education for every single student," Ms. Horne said.

ELEVEN

High SAT and ACT Scores Might Not Spell Success at College

Judy Woodruff and William Hiss

> In the following viewpoint, Judy Woodruff interviews a former college dean of admissions about whether or not standardized test scores really predict a student's ability to succeed in college. The discussion is prompted by results of a study that challenges the value of tried-and-true tests such as the SAT and ACT. The two also discuss whether colleges should stop placing so much weight on test scores when admitting prospective students. Woodruff is an American television news anchor, journalist, and writer who has worked for several television organizations, including CNN, NBC News, and PBS. Hiss is the former dean of admissions at Bates College.

JUDY WOODRUFF: It's one of those times of the year when high school juniors aiming for college are getting ready to take the SAT or the ACT, but a large new study is challenging the value of these well-known standardized tests.

Researchers looked at 33 public and private colleges and universities where it's optional for applicants to submit their test scores. In all, the study examined the records of 123,000 students from more than 20 states. It found that test scores didn't correlate with how well a student did in college based on grades and graduation rates.

The paper has raised a variety of questions from several corners.

Can standardized test performance predict success in college and after graduation?

And we turn to its lead author, William Hiss. He's the former dean of admissions at Bates College in Maine, which is, we should note, a test-optional school.

Bill Hiss, thank you very much for joining us.

First of all, why did you undertake this study?

WILLIAM HISS, Former Dean of Admissions, Bates College: I have been looking at this issue for over 30 years.

I'm trained as an ethicist, so I wasn't trying to find the perfect formula to admit students when I was dean of admissions. Rather, I was trying to say, how do we understand human intelligence? How do we understand promise?

And, originally, we began looking at whether standardized testing helped us to choose talented students or whether it artificially truncated the pools of people who would succeed if we would give them a chance.

JUDY WOODRUFF: And so you were—you had an idea in your mind of what the answer would be before you undertook this?

WILLIAM HISS: Well, we have done at five-year intervals for 30 years studies of the Bates students who were submitters and non-submitters.

JUDY WOODRUFF: Meaning—submitters meaning students who did or didn't submit their test scores.

WILLIAM HISS: Correct. Submit their testing, correct.

And we wanted to do a study that would be a national study. I was frankly surprised to find how closely the national study's results lined up with the long history of studies we have done at Bates.

JUDY WOODRUFF: And so tell us, what were the main findings?

WILLIAM HISS: The main finding is that if students have strong high school records, good grades in high school, their odds of doing well in college are very good even with a quite wide range of testing.

Of the 123,000 students in our study, we had approximately 30 percent who had not submitted their tests or not had them used for admissions decisions. The difference in cumulative GPAs in college turned out to be five-one-hundredths of a GPA point. The difference in graduation rates turned out to be six-tenths of 1 percent.

By any definition, by any statistical standard, those are trivial differences.

JUDY WOODRUFF: So, it's commonly been accepted, though, I

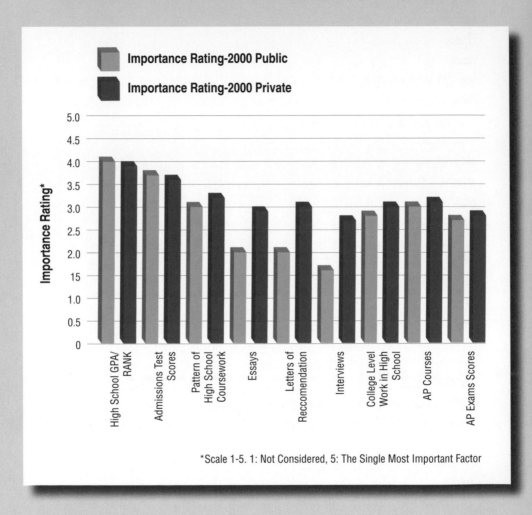

Average importance of various factors in college admissions decisions at four-year public and private institutions, 2000

Importance Rating-2000 Public

Importance Rating-2000 Private

Importance Rating*

5.0
4.5
4.0
3.5
3.0
2.5
2.0
15
1.0
0.5
0

High School GPA/RANK

Admissions Test Scores

Pattern of High School Coursework

Essays

Letters of Reccomendation

Interviews

College Level Work in High School

AP Courses

AP Exams Scores

*Scale 1-5. 1: Not Considered, 5: The Single Most Important Factor

Source: College Board

think, for many years that these tests help in determining whether students should be accepted at college.

What do you think these results should say to colleges that are today insisting that students send in, submit their test results?

WILLIAM HISS: I think that colleges will probably be doing some hopefully analysis of their own predictors college by college. This is a national study, so it looks across institutional types.

Of the 123,000 students in our study, 71,000 were at public universities. Another 12,000 were at minority-serving institutions. We had 20 private colleges and universities in our study. So there's a very wide variety. But I hope institutions will ask themselves the question, would we open up our applicant pools more, would we see larger numbers of students who would succeed if in one way or another we deemphasized the testing?

And that essentially is what Bates has found. Over the years, our applicant pool went from 2,200 to 5,200 for about the same size class. Do you get a better class with two-and-a-half times as many applicants? Of course. Of course you do, and on all the scales, not just academic success, but contributions to the college community in a variety of ways.

JUDY WOODRUFF: What do you say to representatives of the College Board? This is the body that administers the SAT, that they say multiple surveys they have done over the years, tests they have done, evaluations, show that this test is an accurate predictor of college success.

And they also say that—I'm quoting now—"High-quality research shows neither the SAT nor high school grade-point average should be used alone when making college admission decisions."

WILLIAM HISS: Well, I would tend to agree with the second point.

And I would say students should try to show us what they have brought to some high level of success. It may be a viola or debate or soccer goalie or community service. But I agree we should look at more than a single instrument.

I, frankly, was surprised to find how reliable the high school GPA was. And I thought about it a lot. And I myself think that we are looking at two four-year-long demonstrations, high school and college, of self-discipline, curiosity, intellectual drive, if you will, the ability to get your homework done on time, get your papers written.

And so I think there are reasons that the high school GPA turns out to be a very solid predictor. And ours is by far not the first study that has turned up the same results.

JUDY WOODRUFF: And just quickly, finally, pin down for us what harm you see in insisting that students take these tests and submit them.

WILLIAM HISS: Well, the biggest harm is to the country. You truncate the applicant pools of people who would succeed.

And the people who are non-submitters in higher percentages are just who we need to get through, first generation to college, minority students, students with learning disabilities like dyslexia, somewhat more women than men, Pell Grant recipients who are low-income students. These are the people we have to get through college.

So the danger is, you truncate your pool of the people you really need to have in your college.

JUDY WOODRUFF: Bill Hiss, we thank you for talking with us.

WILLIAM HISS: Thank you.

TWELVE

What Colleges Don't Want You to Know About Admissions

Stephen Burd and Rachel Fishman

In the following viewpoint, Stephen Burd and Rachel Fishman present ten ways in which college financial aid and admissions may not be what they seem to be on the surface. Students and their parents must educate themselves on the ways in which colleges manipulate data and information from applications to ensure that they don't make critical mistakes along the way. It's no wonder that so many students rely on savvy guidance counselors and professional consultants to guide them through the process. Burd is a senior policy analyst with the New America Foundation's Education Policy Program. Fishman is a policy analyst for the same program.

#1 Just because a school encourages you to apply doesn't mean they actually want you

High school students who are inundated with personalized letters and emails (and even partially filled-out applications) from colleges urging them to apply may mistakenly think that the institutions contacting them are intending to admit them. In reality, schools often encourage students to apply so that they can reject them.

The aim of the game for colleges is to boost the number of students who apply and can be rejected. By doing this, the schools see their acceptance rates fall, making them appear to be more

"Ten Ways Colleges Work You Over," by Stephen Burd and Rachel Fishman, *Washington Monthly*, September/October 2014. Reprinted by permission.

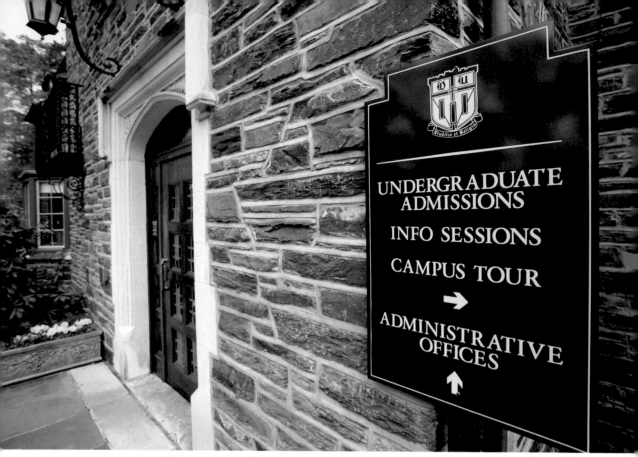

Admissions offices have a lot of tricks up their sleeves, and most of them do not benefit individual students.

selective—which helps them rise up the *U.S. News & World Report* rankings.

Take Northeastern University in Boston. According to a report in the *Wall Street Journal*, the university sends nearly 200,000 personalized letters to high school students each year. The institution then follows up these letters with emails, making it seem that the school is wooing these individuals.

These tactics appear to be paying off. Nearly 50,000 students applied to Northeastern this year for 2,800 spots in the fall 2014 class—"more than in any previous year and a ratio of 18 applicants per seat," the university boasted in a news release.

Lowering its acceptance rates is at least one factor in why Northeastern has catapulted up the *U.S. News* rankings, rising more than 100 spots since 2002.

#2 A college may not be as selective as it seems

Another way that colleges attempt to appear more selective than they really are is through use of the Common Application, a standard form that students can use to easily apply to multiple colleges. Colleges have found that they can use the Common App to inflate their applications in order to lower their acceptance rate—one of the measures used to determine an institution's ranking in *U.S. News*. As it turns out, the proliferation of the Common App has enabled students to easily apply to more than one school even if they are underqualified. Indeed, students are applying to more schools than ever before. In 2000, just a couple of years after the online Common App was introduced, only 12 percent of students applied to seven or more schools; in 2011, 29 percent did.

The University of Chicago provides an example of the factors behind this trend. For years, the university publicly rejected the use of the Common App. In fact, it marketed its own application as the "Uncommon Application." But by 2007, Chicago officials caved to the demands of looking as competitive as the other schools using the Common App. As the vice president and dean of college enrollment told the *Brown Daily* at the time, "We took note of the fact that two of our major competitors, Northwestern and [the University of Pennsylvania], had decided to accept the Common Application."

What was the result of the University of Chicago allowing the Common App? By 2013, the school increased the number of applications it received by more than 20,000 and reduced its acceptance rate by over 24 percentage points. This helped move Chicago from being ranked number nine nationally by U.S. News in 2007 to number five by 2014—ahead of its competitors Northwestern and the University of Pennsylvania.

#3 You may be rejected or wait-listed at a college simply because you are not wealthy

Every year, a substantial number of private colleges reject or wait-list a certain proportion of applicants not because of grades or

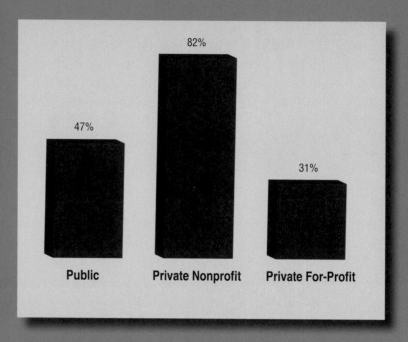

Percentage of students that receive institutional grants at four-year institutions, by type, academic year 2014–2015

82%

47%

31%

Public   Private Nonprofit   Private For-Profit

Source: U.S. Department of Education

test scores or because they would not be a "good fit," but, rather, simply because their families aren't rich enough to pay full freight. These schools, in other words, are "need aware" when admitting a share of their students.

This may seem unjust. But colleges say they have no other choice because they have only a limited amount of money to spend on financial aid. "While financial aid is one of the top three expenditures at Oberlin, the amount of funds available is still finite, and we do have to take that into account in the admissions process," says Elizabeth Houston, who works in the admissions office at Oberlin College.

"If, for instance, we admitted a class comprised entirely of students who could make no financial contribution to their education, we simply couldn't afford it," explains Houston in a blog post on the college's website. "That's an extreme case, but even taking into account the natural mix of income levels a college might see in their applicant pool, there are still very few institutions that are wealthy enough to afford to be completely need-blind and still meet 100 percent of demonstrated need."

According to colleges, this typically doesn't affect low-income students who are at the top of their class. Finances are only taken into account with more marginal students, they say.

Still, in a survey conducted by Inside Higher Ed in 2011, 19 percent of admissions directors at private liberal arts colleges reported that they admit full-pay students with lower grades and test scores than other applicants. These colleges are, in other words, providing affirmative action for the wealthy, despite all of the extraordinary advantages that these students have over their less-fortunate peers.

#4 Low-income students are not always better off at need-blind colleges

It's true that the most elite and wealthiest private colleges, like Harvard University and Amherst College, meet the full demonstrated financial need of their low- and moderate-income students. But many other colleges that boast about being need-blind don't come close. Instead, they leave students with a hefty gap between what the government says they should be expected to pay and what they are being charged.

New York University, for example, admits students regardless of their financial need. However, NYU students from families making $30,000 or less face a daunting average net price—the amount students and their parents must pay after all grant aid has been exhausted—of $24,265 per year. (See "America's Affordable Elite Colleges" page and our full rankings at washingtonmonthly .com, which calculate net price of attendance based on three-year averages.) That means that the lowest-income families are on the hook for an amount that is nearly equal to or even more than their yearly earnings.

Financially needy students who qualify for admission at NYU may actually be better off at "need-aware" schools that meet the full demonstrated need of the low-income students they do enroll.

#5 Need-blind schools are not really blind about their applicants' need

Administrators at purportedly need-blind colleges don't necessarily need to know an applicant's family income to know if he or she is poor, because they have plenty of other clues.

For example, admissions officers know where applicants live and what high school they attended, and whether or not they worked after school or participated in a plethora of extracurricular activities. Admissions staff members also know the occupations of the applicants' parents and whether they attended college, and, more importantly, whether the student is a legacy. And these administrators can learn a lot about students' backgrounds from their college application essays.

So if a need-blind school is looking to admit a much larger share of affluent students for budgetary reasons, it could easily do so without knowing exactly how much an applicant's family earned last year.

#6 It isn't always free to apply for financial aid

Come financial aid season, many students and families realize that they must fill out the Free Application for Federal Student Aid (FAFSA) in order to get a financial aid package from their school. What many families may not realize is that very selective, elite institutions often require a student to fill out another, more extensive form for financial aid. And unlike the FAFSA, this secondary financial aid application—the College Board's CSS/Financial Aid PROFILE—isn't free. The PROFILE is expensive, costing a student $25 just to register and send it to one college, and then $16 for each additional college.

Over the past few years, the U.S. Department of Education has been simplifying the FAFSA in an effort to reduce the barriers that low- and middle-income families face when filling out an unduly complex form. As a result, the number of questions asked on the FAFSA has been reduced, and parents can now use a data-retrieval tool through the IRS to pre-fill answers to many of the questions. These changes have significantly reduced the average time students and families take to complete the application.

But the simplification of the FAFSA has been cause for concern among selective colleges who are hesitant to part with any institutional aid dollars. This has pushed many institutions to require the PROFILE in order to determine institutional aid eligibility. Since FAFSA simplification has removed some questions regarding a family's assets and savings, institutions have adopted the PROFILE to understand exactly how many assets a family owns—including in many instances their house and the make and model of their car—before giving them any aid.

#7 The order that you list colleges on the FAFSA may come back to haunt you

Even if a student is lucky and only has to fill out the FAFSA to get financial aid, he should be wary about the order in which he lists the colleges where he'd like to send the application. According to a recent article in Inside Higher Ed, "Some colleges are denying admissions and perhaps reducing financial aid to students based on a single, non-financial, non-academic question that students submit to the federal government on their [FAFSA]." It turns out that colleges see exactly the order the student listed the schools on the FAFSA and have become savvy at admitting, wait-listing, and packaging aid depending on the student's ordering.

Enrollment managers and management firms—the people charged with figuring out just how many students to admit to "yield" a class—have discovered that students often choose colleges on the FAFSA in preferential order. Inside Higher Ed reported that Augustana College, for example, found that 60 percent of the students who list the school first on the FAFSA end up enrolling, compared with 30 percent of those who list it second, and just 10 percent of those who list it third. Like Augustana, some schools look at a student's "FAFSA position" to determine admissions decisions—completely unbeknownst to the student. A school does this to improve its yield rate, to ensure that it is able to enroll exactly the class it wants.

Some schools may also be taking the "FAFSA position" into account when awarding their own financial aid dollars to students—providing less generous aid packages to students who list the college first on the FAFSA. These colleges don't want to waste precious institutional aid dollars on students who are already likely to attend without the help.

The problem is that not all students necessarily list schools in preferential order, or there may be very little difference among a student's number one, number two, and number three option. Worse yet, the whole process is completely opaque to students. They have no idea that their chances of being admitted and receiving a generous financial aid package may ride largely on the order in which they list schools on the FAFSA.

#8 Financial aid award letters may make options seem more affordable than they really are.

Colleges don't always come clean about how much students and families are going to have to pay to attend an institution. The "financial aid award letters" that colleges send aid applicants they've accepted often make their schools look more affordable than they really are.

One problem is that many colleges and universities package both grants and scholarships with loans and work-study allowances. This blurs how much students and parents are going to owe, often leading them to believe they are getting a great deal when in reality they are taking on a large amount of debt. Some colleges and universities include Parent PLUS loans in the "aid" packages they offer students, in order to bring their purported price down to zero. The Parent PLUS loan, which parents borrow on behalf of their children, come with a higher interest rate and less repayment flexibility than other federal student loans. Additionally, parents have to undergo a credit check to get a Parent PLUS loan. This means that a student and his or her parents may accept the financial aid package, put down a nonrefundable deposit to the institution, and then suddenly find themselves facing steep gaps in financial aid if the parent gets rejected for the loan.

Adding to the confusion over financial aid packages is that each institution has developed its own award letter, making it difficult for students to make an apples-to-apples price comparison among the institutions to which they've been accepted. This could lead them to make a suboptimal choice in terms of which school will provide the best aid package while also still being a good fit academically and socially.

#9 Some aid packages are designed to dissuade you from enrolling.

Many colleges offer extremely generous aid packages to the students they most desire, and leave large funding "gaps" for others in whom they are less interested. In the parlance of enrollment management, this is called "admit-deny," in which schools provide students with aid packages that don't come close to meeting their financial need in order to discourage them from enrolling.

"Admit-deny is when you give someone a financial-aid package that is so rotten that you hope they get the message, 'Don't come,'" Mark Heffron, a senior vice president at the enrollment management firm Noel-Levitz, told the Atlantic Monthly back in 2005. "They don't always get the message."

Under this model, top students receive substantial amounts of grants and either need-based or merit-based scholarships. Those who are less desired have to take on a substantial amount of debt if they want to attend—either through private loans or federal PLUS loans for their parents.

Schools that engage in these practices don't tend to advertise them. An exception is Muhlenberg College, a small private college in Pennsylvania, which includes a page on its website entitled "The Real Deal on Financial Aid."

"It used to be that you could try for that reach school and if you got in, you didn't have to worry because everybody who got in, who needed money, got money," the college's financial aid office states. "Today, however, as colleges are asked to fund more and more of their own operation with less and less assistance from government, foundations, and families, they are increasingly reluctant to part with their money to enroll students who don't raise their academic profile."

#10 Often the financial aid you receive your first year will be less generous the following year

Students and families beware: the plum financial aid package you receive your freshman year may not be quite as impressive your sophomore year. The bait and switch of financial aid packages from year to year is known as "front-loading financial aid." According to Mark Kantrowitz, a financial aid expert, about half of all colleges front-load grants and scholarships so that students receive a bigger discount their first couple of years but then face a financial aid package filled with loans in subsequent years.

Part of the problem is that many parents and students are unaware that they must apply for financial aid every year they are in school and that the price they pay can vary dramatically from year to year. A scholarship may come with a GPA requirement, for example, but it could also just be a one-time award given to incoming freshmen to attract them to the school. Think of it as a signing bonus—or tuition discount—that disappears by year two.

According to a study done by Kantrowitz, enough colleges front-load aid that the average net price for returning students— the price students pay after grants and scholarships are accounted for—is about $1,400 more. He also found that the more selective a college is, the less likely it is that it will front-load grants. What's the best way to figure out if you'll be the victim of a financial aid package bait and switch? Ask the college. Only problem is that some colleges will be less honest than others.

What You Should Know About College Admissions

Facts About Applying to College

- The Common Application, which can be used for applying to about four hundred different schools, does not make it completely easy to apply to many different colleges. Most colleges still require supplemental materials and essays.

- If a student has a first-choice college, he or she should apply using the early decision process. Early decision has been shown to increase the chance of admission by as much as 25 percent over regular decision admission rates.

- Visit a school, including a campus tour and even spending the night if possible, before applying. Schools like to see students visiting before they apply.

- When asking for recommendations for college applications, ask the people who know you best, not the people who seem like they are the most important.

- It takes more than good grades to be accepted at colleges and universities. Testing scores, extracurricular activities, and a written essay are also important.

- Colleges care most about the work you've done in high school. They look for students who have earned strong grades in challenging courses. They also try to learn about your character by looking at what you do outside the classroom.

- Choosing colleges to apply to should be based on how well that college matches your needs and goals, not on how highly it ranks or how prestigious it is.

- Use your family, teachers, friends, school guidance counselor, and even your principal for resources about choosing colleges and navigating financial aid.

Facts About Acceptance

- College admission isn't as competitive as you might think. Fewer than one hundred colleges in the United States are highly selective, which means they accept less than 25 percent of applicants. Almost five hundred four-year colleges accept more than 75 percent of applicants.

- Because colleges want a student body with a good mix of abilities, they tend to look for students who are extremely good in one area rather than fairly good in many areas.

- Of high school seniors, 75 percent are accepted to their first-choice colleges, but less than 57 percent can afford to attend.

- Only 0.4 percent of undergraduates attend one of the Ivy League schools.

- Of the 2,350,000 college students enrolling per year, only 1,750,000 will graduate.

- Each year 775,000 male students enroll in college; 1,575,000 female students enroll each year.

- Admissions officers at colleges will look at everything about a student, including social media. Never post anything online that you wouldn't want to see on the front page of a newspaper or have your family see.

Facts About Attending College

- Anyone who wants to go to college can go to college. There are many different schools, from four-year universities to community colleges, and most schools have expanded the number of students they can enroll.

- The quality of a college education depends on the student, not the school. Students who take advantage of their school's opportunities and take their education seriously will succeed no matter where they attend.

- Getting into college may be a difficult process, but college itself is a wonderful place to explore opportunities and gain specialized knowledge.

What You Should Do About College Admissions

The college admissions process can be difficult and stressful. It requires a good academic record but also testing, writing essays, and getting recommendations from teachers and other adults. However, there are many things that students can do to make the process less stressful. The most important one is to begin planning for college admissions early. Don't wait until the fall of your senior year in high school. Begin taking challenging classes as soon as you start high school, and maintain good grades. Even if your grades start out average, work hard to bring them up. Colleges like to see students who are growing and improving over time. They also like to see students taking difficult courses, not just courses that they can achieve an easy A in. Studying hard and consistently, and not only achieving good grades but also creating good study habits, will pay off both in getting into college and in staying there and being successful. Good study habits can be just as valuable, and sometimes even more valuable, than expensive test prep and college admissions tutoring and courses.

Get involved in extracurricular activities as well as community service projects as early as possible, even before high school. A student who has been taking dance or music lessons or enrichment classes in engineering or inventing since childhood looks good to college admissions officers. A part-time job, involvement with a church or other religious group, volunteering, and even a consistent commitment to caring for a family member or neighbor all demonstrate good qualities that colleges seek in their students.

Again, don't wait until fall of your last year of high school to start thinking about what colleges you'd like to apply to. If you have a clear career goal, you can begin researching colleges to see which ones have strong programs to offer. If you are not sure about what you'd like to do for a career or major in, look for schools with a good mix of majors. Read testimonials from students currently enrolled there or who have graduated and embarked on successful careers. Many schools can match you up with students or graduates in your area that you can speak to in person or someone you can communicate with online. This gives you the opportunity to ask questions about the school and campus life that you might not be able to find online in the college's admissions materials or brochures. Once you have identified schools you'd like to apply to, don't wait until a week or two before applications are due to look for recommendations and write an essay, if required. Leave plenty of time to write and rewrite so that your essay is strong, and have others read it for you. Give the people you're seeking recommendations from plenty of time to write thoughtful letters for you.

The college admissions process is not easy, and it will be stressful no matter what. But you can reduce that stress and increase your chances of finding a school that's right for you and being accepted there if you plan ahead and take plenty of time to complete the process as well as you possibly can.

ORGANIZATIONS TO CONTACT

The editors have compiled the following list of organizations concerned with the issues debated in this book. The descriptions are derived from materials provided by the organizations. All have publications or information available for interested readers. The list was compiled on the date of publication of the present volume; the information provided here may change. Be aware that many organizations take several weeks or longer to respond to inquiries, so allow as much time as possible.

ACT

ACT Test Administration and Accommodations
301 ACT Drive, PO Box 168
Iowa City, IA 52243-0168
(319) 337-1000
email: act@act.org
website: www.act.org/content/act/en.html

The ACT test is the nation's most popular college entrance exam accepted and valued by all universities and colleges in the United States. This site includes everything you need to know about registration, test prep, scores, and more.

College Board

National Office
250 Vesey Street
New York, NY 10281
(212) 713-8000
website: www.collegeboard.org

The College Board is a not-for-profit organization that connects students to college success and opportunity. It helps students prepare for college with programs like the SAT and the Advanced Placement Program.

National Catholic College Admission Association
PO Box 267
New Albany, OH 43054
(614) 633-5444
email: info@nationalccaa.org
website: www.catholiccollegesonline.org

The National Catholic College Admission Association is a nonprofit organization of Catholic colleges and universities committed to promoting the value of Catholic higher education and to serving students, parents, and counselors.

National College Access Network
1001 Connecticut Avenue NW
Suite 300
Washington, DC 20036
(202) 347.4848
email: ncan@collegeaccess.org
website: www.collegeaccess.org

The mission of the National College Access Network is to build, strengthen, and empower communities committed to college access and success so that all students, especially those underrepresented in postsecondary education, can achieve their educational dreams.

National College Fairs
1050 North Highland Street, Suite 400
Arlington, VA 22201
(800)822-6285
email: collegefairs@nacacnet.org
website: www.nacacfairs.org

National College Fairs is a resource provided by the National Association for College Admission Counseling. Through this service, students can find college fair events that can connect them with hundreds of colleges and universities in one location.

The Princeton Review

110 Fieldcrest Ave
Suite 2, 1st Floor
Edison, NJ 08837
(800) 273-8439
website: www.princetonreview.com

The Princeton Review is a series of books, courses, and online resources to help students find colleges and prepare for admissions.

Questbridge

445 Sherman Ave, Suite 100
Palo Alto, CA 94306
(888) 275-2054
questions@questbridge.org
website: www.questbridge.org

QuestBridge is a nonprofit program that links high-achieving, deserving students with educational and scholarship opportunities at leading US colleges and universities.

Upward Bound

Office of Federal TRIO Programs
U.S. Department of Education, OPE
Higher Education Programs
Upward Bound Program
400 Maryland Avenue SW
Washington, DC 20202
(202) 453-6273
website: www2.ed.gov/programs/trioupbound/index.html

Upward Bound provides fundamental support to participants in their preparation for college entrance. Upward Bound serves high school students from low-income families and high school students from families in which neither parent holds a bachelor's degree.

Books

Deborah Bedor, *Getting IN by Standing OUT: The New Rules for Admission to America's Best Colleges.* Charleston, SC: Advantage Media Group, 2015.
This book offers strategies for getting into prestigious colleges.

Frank Bruni, *Where You Go Is Not Who You'll Be: An Antidote to the College Admissions Mania.* New York, NY: Grand Central Publishing, 2016.
An exploration of the college admissions process today and why it is flawed.

Pria Chatterjee, *The Dirty Little Secrets of Getting Into a Top College.* New York, NY: Regan Arts, 2015.
A top college admissions insider exposes the never-before revealed secrets to getting into one of America's elite colleges.

Carol Christen, *What Color Is Your Parachute? for Teens, Third Edition: Discover Yourself, Design Your Future, and Plan for Your Dream Job.* Emeryville, CA: Ten Speed Press, 2015.
A guide to help high school and college students zero in on their favorite skills and find their perfect major or career.

The College Board, *Get It Together For College, 4th Edition.* New York, NY: The College Board, 2017.
This planner covers everything students need to know about getting organized for college applications.

Alan Gelb, *Conquering the College Admissions Essay in 10 Steps, Third Edition: Crafting a Winning Personal Statement.* Emeryville, CA: Ten Speed Press, 2017.
An easy-to-follow but comprehensive guide to considering and crafting a solid college application essay.

Fredrick C. Harris and Robert C. Lieberman, *Beyond Discrimination: Racial Inequality in a Postracist Era.* New York, NY: Russell Sage Foundation, 2013.
In this eye-opening book, a diverse group of scholars offers viewpoints on understanding racial inequality in American institutions, including education.

The Princeton Review, *The Complete Book of Colleges, 2018 Edition*. Edison, NJ: The Princeton Review, 2017.
An annual guide to all the colleges and universities in the United States that offers detailed user profiles to help students determine the best college for them.

Sally P. Springer, Jon Reider, and Joyce Vining Morgan, *Admission Matters: What Students and Parents Need to Know About Getting into College*. New York, NY: Jossey-Bass, 2017.
A comprehensive guide to the college admission process, offering perspectives for both parents and students.

Lois Weis, Kristin Cipollone, and Heather Jenkins, *Class Warfare: Class, Race, and College Admissions in Top-Tier Secondary Schools*. Chicago, IL: The University of Chicago Press, 2014.
The authors interview students, parents, and college admissions officers to unveil a formidable process of class positioning at the heart of the college admissions process.

Rebecca Zwick, *Who Gets In?: Strategies for Fair and Effective College Admissions*. Cambridge, MA: Havard University Press, 2017.
This examination of the college admissions process considers the merits and flaws and demonstrates that admissions policies can sometimes fail to produce the desired results.

Periodicals and Internet Sources

Frank Bruni, "How to Survive the College Admissions Madness." *New York Times*, March 13, 2015. https://www.nytimes.com/2015/03/15/opinion/sunday/frank-bruni-how-to-survive-the-college-admissions-madness.html?_r=0.

Frank Bruni, "Rethinking College Admission," *New York Times* ,January 13, 2015. https://www.nytimes.com/2016/01/20/opinion/rethinking-college-admissions.html.

Matt Feeney, "The Poisonous Reach of the College-Admissions Process." *New Yorker*, January 28, 2016. http://www.newyorker.com/culture/cultural-comment/the-poisonous-reach-of-the-college-admissions-process.

Tyler Hakes, "Why College Admissions Won't Be Changing Any Time Soon." College Raptor. Accessed July 13, 2017. https://www.collegeraptor.com/find-colleges/articles/college-news-trends/why-college-admissions-wont-be-changing-any-time-soon.

Judy Mandell, "What College Admissions Officers Say They Want in a Candidate." *Washington Post*, August 30, 2016. https://www.washingtonpost.com/news/parenting/wp/2016/08/30/what-21-college-admissions-officers-say-they-want-in-a-candidate/?utm_term=.78092d1e32ea.

Farran Powell, "How Competitive Is College Admissions?" *Washington Post*, September 22, 2016. https://www.usnews.com/education/best-colleges/articles/2016-09-22/how-competitive-is-college-admissions.

Danny Ruderman, "The College Admissions Process Is Broken." *US News and World Report*, June 29, 2017. https://www.usnews.com/opinion/knowledge-bank/articles/2017-06-19/the-college-application-process-works-for-no-one.

Jeffrey J. Selingo, "Let's End the Craziness of College Admissions." *Washington Post*, January 20, 2017. https://www.washingtonpost.com/news/grade-point/wp/2017/01/20/lets-end-the-craziness-of-college-admissions/?utm_term=.5d4fdfe1a9fb.

Laura Stampler, "How High School Students Use Instagram to Help Pick a College." *Time Magazine*, April 2, 2015. http://time.com/3762067/college-acceptance-instagram-high-school.

Valerie Strauss, "Five myths about college admissions." *Washington Post*, March 24, 2017. https://www.washingtonpost.com/opinions/five-myths-about-college-admissions/2017/03/24/673a03a2-0f2a-11e7-9d5a-a83e627dc120_story.html?utm_term=.26d33867fbbd.

Alia Wong, "The Absurdity of College Admissions." *Atlantic*, March 28, 2016. https://www.theatlantic.com/education/archive/2016/03/where-admissions-went-wrong/475575.

Alia Wong, "Where College Admissions Went Wrong." *Atlantic*, March 29, 2016. https://www.theatlantic.com/education/archive/2016/03/college-admissions-narcissists/475722.

Websites

ACT (http://www.act.org/content/act/en.html)

This site contains information about the ACT test, one of the most popular college entrance exams used by all universities and colleges in the United States.

College Board (https://www.collegeboard.org)

The College Board is a not-for-profit organization that helps students prepare for college. The site contains information about the SAT and the Advanced Placement Program.

Princeton Review (https://www.princetonreview.com)

This company provides college information, test prep, and other college admissions resources.

INDEX